From Generation *to* Generation

From Generation *to* Generation

The Adaptive Challenge of Mainline Protestant
Education in Forming Faith

CHARLES R. FOSTER

CASCADE *Books* • Eugene, Oregon

FROM GENERATION TO GENERATION
The Adaptive Challenge of Mainline Protestant Education in Forming Faith

Cascade Books
An Imprint of Wipf and Stock Publishers
199 W. 8th Ave., Suite 3
Eugene, OR 97401

www.wipfandstock.com

ISBN 13: 978-1-62032-195-9

Cataloging-in-Publication data:

Foster, Charles R.

From generation to generation: the adaptive challenge of mainline Protestant education in forming faith / Charles R. Foster.

viii + 150 p.; 23 cm—Includes bibliographical references.

ISBN 13: 978-1-62032-195-9

1. Christian Education. 2. Christianity—Forecasting. 3. Church work. I. Title.

BV1464 .F68 2012

Manufactured in the USA.

I dedicate this book to those whose ecclesial educational imaginations ensure a future for their religious traditions through the faith of their children and youth.

Contents

Introduction

Every community that wants to last beyond a single generation must concern itself with education.

—WALTER BRUEGGEMANN, *The Creative Word*

Lament

About the time I initiated this writing project I had the opportunity to speak to a group of women who belonged to a congregation of one of the old mainline Protestant denominations. We talked informally as the group gathered. I discovered most had grown up in the denominational tradition of that congregation. They had participated in its youth ministries. They went on to college, married, and raised families. They took their children to Sunday school and encouraged them to participate in the congregation's youth fellowship. With one exception, all were now grandmothers with a deep interest in and concern for the future of their grandchildren.

They had invited me to discuss a study of clergy education I had directed for the Carnegie Foundation for the Advancement of Teaching.[1] They asked thoughtful questions about the students I had met, their classes, and other parts of the seminary curriculum. The discussion had not gone long, however, before I realized their interest had deeper roots. They wanted to know what I had to say about the pastoral leaders they could anticipate in the future. They especially wanted to know if the seminary students we en-

---

1. Charles R. Foster and others, *Educating Clergy*.

1

countered possessed sufficient faith and knowledge, vision and skill to lead congregations like theirs. The impetus to their interest began with a lament. This lament originated in a gap between their memories of the lively role of the church in their lives as children and youth during the 1950s and early 1960s and the comparative lack of significance it had, in most instances, for their children, and now for their grandchildren.

The depths of their lament increased as they described how few children and youth were participating in their congregation and other congregations of the mainline Protestant denominations with which they were most familiar.[2] They raised questions I had heard before in other groups of loyal middle-aged and older adults in congregations linked to the denominations of the old Protestant mainline: "Why don't we have more children and youth in our church?" "Why don't more of the children we do have remain active during adolescence and after they graduate from high school?" "Why haven't those who left as young adults returned to our churches after they married and had children of their own?" Then back to a theme running through their comments, "Why don't our pastors pay more attention to young people?" And ultimately, "why aren't seminaries training clergy to work more effectively with young people?"

At one point the discussion became quite personal. They described difficulties they experienced as parents during the 1970s, 1980s, and 1990s in sustaining the interest of their own children in the religious heritages of the congregations they attended. Some described their children's general resistance to the church and its ministries. Others talked about the preference of their teenagers for a para-church youth group in the community. They all identified challenges they faced as parents and as a congregation in competing for time with school activities and other youth programs in the community. Most admitted their children as adults had either moved on to one of the large and often non-denominational evangelical congregations near where they lived or had disassociated themselves entirely from any formal religious organization. "What happened?" they wanted to know. "Would a different kind of pastoral leadership have made any difference?"

What happened? For close to thirty years now clergy and laity alike have been asking me that question in one form or another in workshops I have led and in private conversations. I heard it often enough to compare

---

2. In the community where they lived old mainline Protestant congregations were associated with United Methodist, AME Zion, United Church of Christ, Presbyterian Church USA, Episcopal, American Baptist, Evangelical Lutheran Church of America, and Disciples of Christ denominations.

my childhood experience in congregations of an old mainline denomination with that of our daughter and grandchildren in congregations of that same denomination. Through my research and writing, I struggled to make sense of the deliberations I observed in local churches, judicatories, and national boards and committees about curriculum, leadership development, and educational strategies for the nurture of faith. Some form of that question increasingly influenced my decisions about what to teach in seminary classrooms and workshops with local church leaders.

Along the way I realized others were asking similar questions about both the public and religious education of children and youth not only in the United States but in places like Canada and Australia. Catalysts to their inquiries were many and varied, including among others:

- the response of communities to the racial integration of their public schools;

- the shift of emphasis in public schools from educating future citizens to educating future producers and consumers—a shift at the heart of a Carnegie study of high schools called *The Shopping Mall High School*;[3]

- the increasingly public mission of Catholic parochial schools;

- the outsourcing of the formation of family values and practices to childcare institutions, preschools, and programmatic movements like *Focus on the Family*;

- the increasing identification of citizenship with discipleship education in a growing number of schools associated with evangelical Protestantism;

- and the shift to marketing strategies for curriculum resources in mainline denominations as publishing houses sought to accommodate conflicting expectations in their constituencies over what to teach and how.

I also discovered many scholars and church leaders were seeking to understand in more general terms the changing landscape of the nation and its religious communities after the 1950s. The focus of their attention may be seen in a random sample of the titles of their works: Herberg's *Protestant, Catholic, Jew*; Whyte's *Organization Man*; Reisman's *The Lonely Crowd*; and Winter's *The Suburban Captivity of the Church*. The quest of a more recent generation of scholars increasingly focused on the status and role of organized religion in the nation, as seen in Roof and McKinney's *American*

---

3. Powell et al., *The Shopping Mall High School*.

Mainline Religion; Wuthnow's *The Struggle for America's Soul*; Roof's *Generation of Seekers* and his *Spiritual Marketplace*; Beaudoin's *Virtual Faith*; Jacoby's *Age of Unreason*; the influential inquiry by Robert Bellah and his colleagues into the *Habits of the Heart in American Life*; the recent study of *American Grace: How Religion Divides and Unites Us*, by Robert Putnam and David Campbell; and the focused attention of Diana Butler Bass on the recent struggles of mainline Protestant churches in *Christianity for the Rest of Us* and *Christianity after Religion*. Their insights highlight the shifting cultural landscape in which the religious communities of the nation and the churches of the Protestant mainline denominations in particular found themselves. They explore declining numbers and vitality along with diminishing denominational loyalty. They describe institutional innovations and emerging forms of leadership. They trace the collapse of their cultural and political influence. They identify challenges in the changing landscape of American life for denominational leaders in national and judicatory offices and pastors and lay leaders in congregations.

My questions led me in a different and more focused direction. I wanted to understand how congregations in the historically mainline Protestant denominations had responded to challenges these scholars were describing. I was curious about how they made sense of and engaged the changing religious and cultural contexts in which they found themselves. This line of inquiry eventually led to another question lurking beneath the surface of the one posed by this group of women: *Why, during the latter decades of the twentieth century, did the denominations of the old Protestant mainline generally cease to envision a lively and robust future for themselves through the children in their congregations?* The question can be stated more boldly. *Why did the denominations of the Protestant mainline give up on a commitment to education at the heart of their liturgies of infant baptism or dedication?* That commitment is articulated forcefully, for example, in a congregational vow at the conclusion of a baptismal liturgy frequently used in congregations of my own denomination:

> **Pastor**: *Members of the household of faith, I commend to your love and care this child, whom we this day recognize as a member of the family of God. Will you endeavor so to live that this child may grow in the knowledge and love of God, through our Savior Jesus Christ?*
>
> **Congregation**: *With God's help we will so order our lives after the example of Christ, that this child, surrounded by steadfast love, may*

be established in the faith, and confirmed and strengthened in the
way that leads to life eternal.[4]

An Adaptive Challenge Proposal

In the pages that follow I ask what it might require, at this point in time, for congregations of the old Protestant mainline to fulfill their commitments to "so order their lives after the example of Christ" as to "establish," "confirm," and "strengthen" the faith of their baptized children and youth.[5] I do so with the hope that others will take up the task of understanding the larger picture of what happened more generally to the expectations of the nation's religious communities about their role and place in forming the lives and faith of their children and youth. I begin with a discussion of education in forming faith. That leads me to ask what happened during the latter decades of the twentieth century to the "ordered life" in the education of mainline Protestant congregations for establishing, confirming, and strengthening the faith of children and youth. In the remaining three chapters I then offer a constructive proposal for a view of and approach to education—specifically, a Christian religious education—that might be both large enough and specific enough to ground this baptismal promise once again in practices that cultivate and sustain the faith of children and youth.

I ground the argument for this proposal in the juxtaposition of a reading of history and a commitment to the continuing vitality and relevance of the traditions of faith embedded in the old mainline Protestant denominations. That reading led me to conclude that as these *denominations encountered cultural challenges to their identities and mission in the decades after World War II, they largely abandoned commitments to education as a means to envision a lively and robust future for themselves through their children and youth.* Congregations have not ceased their educational *programs* or *activities.* They maintain Sunday schools, sponsor youth groups, and organize

4. *United Methodist Hymnal*, 44.

5. This question is also relevant to the future of evangelical Protestant, Roman Catholic, and Orthodox congregations. Their stories are not told here, however, because significant differences exist in their approaches to forming the faith of their children and youth. The stories of the collapse, in some instances, and diminishment, in others, of their approaches to faith formation must be told by those more familiar with them than am I. The adaptive challenges they face in forming the faith of their children and youth, however, have many similarities to those facing congregations of the old mainline Protestant denominations.

adults into a wide variety of learning groups. Denominational publishing houses continue to develop and publish curriculum resources. Judicatories still offer workshops for teachers and leaders. These efforts, however, gradually lost support and reinforcement in the old mainline Protestant denominations as they systematically dismantled the institutional structures aligning education in the congregation with the purposes and strategies of education in the denomination. I have found little evidence church leaders intended to abandon their commitments to education in forming the faith of their children and youth. Rather it happened as they:

- attempted to respond to critiques of the continuing relevance and influence of their ministries in the changing cultural landscape of the nation, in works such as Gibson Winter's *Suburban Captivity of the Church,* Ralph Morton's *God's Frozen People,* and Peter Berger's *The Noise of Solemn Assemblies*;

- struggled with the racism and sexism embedded in their structures in the midst of the civil rights movement;

- attempted to manage the impact of what Robert Putnam and David Campbell describe as the increasing pluralization and polarization of American religion over matters of belief, authority, and morality;[6]

- encountered both the volatility and creativity of the "youth movements" associated with but not limited to the protests of young people to the war in Vietnam and their challenges to traditional moral values related to sexuality;

- were caught up in cultural forces shifting expectations of religious belonging in what Wade Clark Roof and William McKinney call the "new voluntarism" in American religion, distinguished by "greater choice in religious affiliation" and a "more privatized psychology of religious faith and identity."[7]

During these years denominations restructured, and in some instances restructured over and again, their institutional support structures for the education of congregations. They drastically reduced programs for training professional and volunteer leaders in congregational education. Their

---

6. Putnam and Campbell, *American Grace,* 2–4. They point out that the pluralization of American religion included both the proliferation of religious options within Christianity and the growing presence of other religious traditions, including among others Islam, Buddhism, and Hinduism.

7. Roof and McKinney, *American Mainline Religion,* 9.

publishing houses increased curriculum options often by collaborating on their development and production with each other. At the same time non-denominational freelance religious education entrepreneurs published an ever expanding array of alternative curriculum and programmatic resources and training opportunities. Para-church organizations produced new and often more accessible resources and programs for training youth ministry leaders and teachers.

Thoughtful people in congregations, national church agencies, and theological schools meanwhile struggled to understand how to cultivate the faith of children and youth in this changing cultural context and expanding marketplace of religious education resources and strategies. Their quests led many to focus attention on new insights about spiritual formation, faith development, practical theology, and spiritual practices as alternative ways of envisioning the processes of forming faith.[8] These new developments however, have not generally linked questions about forming personal faith to challenges of equipping congregations "for the work of ministry" in "building up the body of Christ" into "the unity of the faith and of the knowledge of the Son of God," in the traditions of the Reformation in a radically and rapidly changing world.[9]

This brings us back to my primary observation. Lost in this new marketplace of religious education options was a notion of education as a theological practice in the denominations of the Protestant mainline adequate to the tasks of maintaining and renewing the faith of their congregations through their children and youth. The focus of my attention is on education in congregations, but historically that education has been inextricably linked to notions of Christian religious education embedded in their denominational heritages and conducted through denominational program agencies and curriculum resources. With the dismantling of denominational structures and the proliferation of their resources, congregations seeking a future for themselves through their children were generally abandoned by their denominational education agencies.[10] They were now confronted

---

8. I generalize here. The extent of the dismantling of these integrative educational structures and processes varied from denomination to denomination. The catechism, for example, continues to provide a shared formative experience for many Evangelical Lutherans.

9. Eph 4:12–14 (New Revised Standard Version).

10. Theda Skocpal explores the collapse of the supporting and reinforcing bonds linking local organizations (including congregations) and their "larger collectivities" (in this instance, their denominations) in *Diminished Democracy*. Note especially her

with an overwhelming challenge. This challenge could not be met by a new program or curriculum, although they were often tried; rather it required large changes in how congregations and their denominations imagined and conducted a faith-forming education among their children and youth to extend and renew their faith traditions into the future.

Ronald Heifetz and Marty Linsky call this an adaptive rather than a technical challenge.[11] The distinction is important. Technical challenges can usually be addressed with existing knowledge, "know-how and procedures." Adaptive challenges require knowledge, know-how, and procedures we do not yet have. Facing a technical challenge, we can rely on the authority of prior experience. That is not the case with an adaptive challenge. We need to be engaged in "experiments, new discoveries and adjustments" to account for losses that inevitably result from our "changing attitudes, values, and behaviors."

Engaging the unknown in an adaptive challenge involves risk. Some risks are obvious while others remain hidden. Changes embedded in our adaptations are just as likely to be painful as helpful. Introducing a new curriculum resource or adopting a new strategy, time, or place for teaching and learning, in other words, will not alone revive a moribund educational ministry. Something at once more radical and expansive is needed. In the pages that follow I will argue that this adaptive challenge engages congregations and their denominations in three critical tasks.

The first involves reclaiming a notion of learning conducive to forming faith in the education of congregations. Specifically it calls for congregations once again to embrace the interdependence of what I will be calling developmental, practice, and discovery learning. These are not new terms. Educational strategies attentive to developmental learning have long emphasized the expanding readiness of children and youth for increasingly complex learning tasks. Most contemporary curriculum resources take these patterns of readiness in developmental learning seriously. Educational strategies attentive to discovery learning emphasize the environment of learning as a playground of possibility for curious and inventive minds. Leadership training programs in old mainline Protestant denominations generally encouraged Sunday school teachers and youth leaders to be open to student questions and encourage curiosity. Educational strategies

---

discussion of "Local and Intimate Solidarities" in face to face groups and the influence of being "Part of Something Bigger," 78–89.

11. Heifetz and Linsky, *Leadership on the Line*, 13–14.

attentive to practice learning emphasize the cultivation of competencies young people need to identify with and participate fully in the religious tradition of a congregation. Each approach to learning has a primary role in a faith-forming education. Each is diminished if one or another is not emphasized. When the old mainline Protestant denominations dismantled their educational infrastructure, however, their congregations paid less and less attention to the role of practice learning in their education. It should be no surprise then that children and youth who have not become proficient in the practices of the faith of some congregation or religious tradition would no longer identify with its heritage or mission.

A second task involves revitalizing congregations as catechetical cultures of faith formation and transformation. By drawing attention to what I am calling the catechetical culture of congregations, I am highlighting the interplay of formal and informal social processes and practices in congregational life that maintain and renew their visions, values, and practices through the generations. Contemporary congregational cultures of faith formation, however, tend to be extremely fragile. The pluralism of religious and secular ideology and practice disrupt the coherence and stability of congregational life. The continuing explosion of knowledge renders difficult making judgments about what should be taught to extend the identity and vocation of a congregation into the future. Hierarchical assumptions about teaching and learning inherited from the past inhibit the impetus to faith and constrain the learning entailed by the journey of faith in our rapidly changing world. In this situation, the adaptive challenge for congregations in forming faith requires renewed attention to cultural patterns and practices that sustain, reinforce, and renew their educational efforts.

I therefore suggest the catechetical culture that nurtures and sustains a faith-forming education is not predominantly an institutional or ideological reality as much as it is a relational dynamic. Hospitable spaces for its practices of teaching and learning must be created. The times have to be chosen. The relationships have to be nurtured. I believe those places and times potentially exist in many of the *events* currently listed on the calendars of every congregation. I am especially intrigued by the formative potential in the liturgical and missional events deeply rooted in their traditions that give them their distinctive shape and purpose. C. Ellis Nelson, back in 1967, underscored their importance when he described them as the "units of life in which past revelation and present experience are united," thereby becoming "the building blocks out of which we erect our life of faith."[12] When congregations expand their attention to educating for empowered celebration in and through these events, they become catalysts to the informal and formal conversations that bind, in turn, the diversity of a congregation's children, youth, and adults into a community of faith.

A third task involves the cultivation of an ecclesially grounded educational imagination in congregations. For the most part in recent years, the old mainline Protestant denominations and their congregations have viewed this adaptive challenge as a technical one. They developed new curriculum resources. They created alternative strategies for teaching and learning. They proposed different settings and times throughout the week and in a variety of places. Many of these efforts have been creative but none has been caught up in a groundswell of educational transformation within or across the denominations of the old Protestant mainline.[13] The structure of the *school* with its *lessons, teachers,* and *students* typically in age-designated *classes* continues to dominate the imaginations of church leaders from congregation to denominational education agencies. Something more is needed; something that expands our attention from the school of the church to the celebrative events punctuating the common life of the congregation throughout the year; from the authority of designated leaders to the creativity of a congregation's responsiveness to the redemptive and creative love of God; from the separation of the generations to their interdependence. That imaginative capacity, I argue, already exists in most congregations as they prepare for and participate in the *events* that hold and give meaning to their life together. In our preparation for, participation in, and reflection back on the celebration of these events we may discover once again the imaginative resources for transmitting a congregation's faith across the generations.

We are not the first generation confronted with the adaptive challenge of finding an education adequate to the task of forming the faith of our children and youth. A model for our efforts may be found in the ancient

---

12. Nelson, *Where Faith Begins*, 95.

13. This does not mean there has been no conversation. Indeed, to the contrary, a lively conversation about the religious and spiritual issues of young people and the church's ministry with young people does exist, unfortunately however, for the most part on the margins of more general church discussions. Mainline Protestant and Catholic participants with published works include Dori Baker, Kenda Creasy Dean, Fred Edie, Brian Mahan, Bonnie Miller McLemore, Joyce Mercer, Evelyn Parker, Don Richter, Katherine Turpin, David White, and Karen-Marie Yust. Their works are cited in the bibliography.

traditions associated with the Passover meal. In this annual re-echoing or rehearsal of the story of the Exodus from Egypt, a child asks the question that prompts the telling and retelling of that story. It is not just any story. It is the story that includes every Jewish child who participates in this practice. It is not just the telling of the story. It is the conversation that recalls prior times when the story was told, interprets its significance for the situation in which those telling the story find themselves, and anticipates future times in different circumstances when the story will be told again. Neither is it limited to the conversations about the story. Practices associated with the story embody its meaning in the relationships and activities of the community whose life is rooted in the story. The telling of that story, the conversations surrounding its telling, and the practices extending the story into the routines of daily life are all crucial. If our children do not know stories of our ancestors' faith well enough to live into their meanings and purposes, who will tell them to the next generation?

My Stance

I need to be candid about my relationship to this discussion. I do not approach the questions and topics explored in the pages that follow as an objective observer or disinterested researcher. I am first of all an insider to what happened to Christian religious education in the old mainline Protestant denominations. I grew up in a congregation of one of those denominations and was active as a youth and then college student leader in its judicatory programs. I graduated from an ecumenical seminary with a course of study taught by an internationally prominent faculty from several Protestant denominations. After graduating I, along with most of my peers, began my ministry in a congregation of one of the old mainline Protestant denominations at the height of their cultural and religious influence in the life of the nation. I was called its Minister of Education. I had specific responsibility for the oversight of that congregation's educational ministry with children, youth, and adults. I was trained to lead workshops and practice-oriented laboratory schools for teachers and leaders of youth in congregations across the country. I returned to graduate school to pursue questions about tensions I had experienced during my ministry in that congregation between church and public school in the education of children and youth.

I spent the next thirty-plus years helping prepare seminary students for the leadership of congregational ministries of education and exploring with them educational issues at the intersection of religion and the cultural life of the nation. During that time I wrote curriculum resources for my denomination and participated in a wide variety of denominational and ecumenical program and policy discussions about the future of the church's ministries with children and youth. Every so often I would take up the challenge of trying to make sense of the increasing confusion in church policies and programs for children and youth. I was especially drawn to issues involving race and ethnicity, the function of our faith traditions for being faithful in the present, and the role of young people in the life of the church. I would research the issue and write an essay for publication or prepare a lecture for a conference. Over and again I was intrigued by the contrast I experienced between the lively discussions these articles evoked and the lack of their impact on the decisions in denominations about their educational policies and resources.

Although I am now retired from my seminary teaching post, I continue to lead workshops, speak to church groups about the educational mission of the church, and work with teachers and leaders in the congregation my wife and I attend. The dynamics of continuity and change in the formation of our lives and religious communities still dominate my attention. Questions about how congregations draw on their faith traditions to envision a future responsive to the challenges of a rapidly changing world continue to give focus to my work. I approach these questions from the vantage point of my training as a historian and practical theologian. I am intrigued by the persistent influence of some ideas, practices, customs, institutions, and some people on the imaginations of communities from one generation into the next. In this regard I stand in the tradition of my teachers and mentors Larry Cremin at Teachers College-Columbia University, and Ellis Nelson and Bob Lynn at Union Theological Seminary.[14]

14. Lawrence A. Cremin taught the history of American education at Teachers College-Columbia University for a number of years before becoming the president of that institution. His writing significantly shifted the discourse about American education away from a preoccupation with schooling to the place of schooling in what he called a "configuration" of educational agencies and institutions, including but not limited to family, church, school, magazines and journals, newspapers and tracts, etc. He spelled out his views in a popular little book entitled *The Genius of American Education*. C. Ellis Nelson and Robert W. Lynn taught at Union Theological Seminary across the street from Teachers College. Nelson's *Where Faith Begins*, in a similar move shifted our attention from the school as agency of faith formation to the congregation in which the school

Following their lead, I assume meanings associated with any experience or practice originate in the encounter of our collective pasts and shared future. This suggests they take form in the responses of our ancestors to events and circumstances deeply rooted in their own real and imagined pasts. This should be a familiar observation for Christians. We live in the wake of being liberated from slavery in the Exodus and the establishment of a new community in a "promised land," being taken captive into Babylon and the creation of an alternative community in exile, encountering in Jesus new possibilities for the life of faith and forming congregations as his followers under the thumb of Roman rule, discovering anew the power of the biblical witness in the midst of the conflicts of the Reformation and Counter Reformation, establishing with the Puritans and Franciscans new communities in a *new* but also quite ancient world, all the while, coming to terms with the influence of new technologies and changing social and cultural expectations. We also live more immediately in the wake of our own responses to the confluence of our memories of events like these from the past and images of the future we seize from them to make sense of the events and circumstances of our own lives.

From another angle, my training in practical theology emphasized theories and practices typically identified with the field of religious or Christian religious education. I struggled, however, with the capacity in that phrase to connect my vocational calling to the work I envisioned for myself in ministry. It did not adequately convey for me the emphasis on theologizing *in* practices of forming and transforming faith I developed for that ministry under the tutelage of Eugene Laubach, my seminary field education supervisor, John Casteel, the director of field education at Union Theological Seminary, and Thomas Steen, my colleague and mentor in my first pastoral appointment.[15] Then I found in J. Stanley Glen's notion of the *ministry of teaching* a language that described more fully a way of linking my sense of vocation to my work in ministry.

---

was located. Robert Lynn's *Protestant Strategies of Education* argued that one could not understand the formation of Protestant faith in the United States without understanding the interdependence of the Sunday and public school in that process.

15. In field education supervisory groups led by Eugene E. Laubach, Minister of Education at the Methodist Church in Westfield, New Jersey and later at the Riverside Church in New York City and in classes with John Casteel at Union Theological Seminary, I was introduced to the practice of critical theological reflection in practice. Thomas Steen, my senior colleague on the staff of First Methodist Church in Corning, New York, continued to engage me in this practice as we reflected on the ministries of that congregation.

The teaching ministry, he argued, "interpenetrates all other ministries." Its primary concerns are to make the Bible and traditions of Christian faith more intelligible and to increase their relevance for the challenges we face in living from day to day. Its primary task is to mediate the "offensiveness" of the gospel by cultivating the kind of thinking that takes seriously both its truth and grace. This kind of thinking, in the words of the apostle Paul, leads not to conformity with the world, but to a transformation of consciousness through the "renewal" of our minds in the quest to discern "the will of God" so we might then embrace "what is good, and acceptable and perfect."[16] Glen locates this model for thinking in the "conversations of Jesus which although deeply theological were couched in the language of concreteness and conducive to response."[17]

Glen's vision of the teaching ministry redirected my attention from educational programs, agencies, and resources to educational practices of faith formation and transformation. This shift highlights what Jean Lave and Etienne Wenger identify as "the relational character of knowledge and learning," the "negotiated character of meaning," and the "concerned (engaged, dilemma-driven) nature" of the historical and social *situatedness* of our activities.[18] It emphasizes the formative influence of ecclesial practices and the theologies embedded in those practices in the formation of faith from generation to generation. To paraphrase the seminal work of Chris Argyris and Donald Schön, it highlights theological reflection *in* faith forming educational practices.[19]

Again, these should be familiar insights to many who have grown up in some mainstream Protestant congregation. They would have probably been introduced at an early age to the song "Jesus Loves Me." They would have sung it in Sunday school classes, in assemblies and worship services, often while at play, and sometimes with youth and adults. Over the course of their lives it may well have become one of the songs of faith they most frequently sing. The tune is memorable. The words make a profoundly accessible theological statement. Its repetition reinforces the message of Jesus' love. As they began to read stories of Jesus in the Bible they might have discovered clues to what that love entails. Experiences of unconditional love in

---

16. Romans 12:2.

17. Glen, *The Recovery of the Teaching Ministry*, 29, 34–35.

18. Lave and Wenger, *Situated Learning*, 33.

19. Argyris and Schön distinguish between the theories we espouse and those embedded in what we do in *Theory in Practice*, vii–viii.

family and congregation may have given credence to the character of that love. Encounters with mistrust, discrimination, and oppression might have thwarted its message, challenging them at whatever age to rethink how they were to relate to and make sense of that love. In their experience of singing this little song over and again, reflecting on the meaning of its words, and imagining its influence on their lives we may begin to envision something of the trajectory that makes up a faith-forming education.

Audience

In 1963, when I graduated from seminary, the publisher of a book like this one would have been clear about its audience. It would have included several thousand professionally trained lay and ordained Christian educators, youth and children's workers working full-time in congregations and judicatories, national denominational agencies, and publishing houses as editors of curriculum resources. It would have included hundreds of students in colleges and seminaries anticipating careers in these settings, their teachers, along with large networks of trained and certified volunteer leaders of denominational training programs variously called laboratory schools, workshops, and coaching conferences who promoted the sale of books like this one. Other potential readers would have included policy and program committee members in congregations and judicatories with deep and long-term commitments to the values of education in the churches. None of these audiences exist to any extent today. Denominational support for theologically trained Christian educators, youth and children's workers declined and in some instances, collapsed in the late 1970s and early 1980s. Jobs disappeared or were transformed to emphasize managerial skills rather than the interplay of theological and pedagogical knowledge. Many seminaries did not replace retiring faculty in the field and discarded courses they had once taught. The remaining graduate professional schools with the special mission of educating future generations of Christian educators either were closed (e.g., Scarritt Graduate School) or were absorbed into a seminary program (e.g., Presbyterian School of Christian Education). Denominational programs for the training and support of volunteer teachers and leaders were dismantled. Congregations and judicatories soon discovered they no longer had a pool of knowledgeable advocates for their educational ministries and publishers faced the reality of a diminishing audience of readers for books on the shape and future of the field.

In the midst of the reality of this situation four groups of potential readers have been much on my mind. Each group brings a different set of expectations to the questions I am exploring. Each also has a shared interest in the continuing relevance of our different religious traditions for living in our rapidly changing world. Each is crucial, moreover, in any constructive conversation about the adaptive challenge of educating for faith in the congregations of the old mainline Protestant denominations and the contributions of Christian communities of faith to public discussions of contemporary social, political, and economic issues.

The first group includes pastors and persons professionally responsible for the oversight of education in historic Protestant mainline congregations, judicatories, and denominations; curriculum writers and producers responsible for producing resources for the educational ministries of congregations; as well as college and seminary professors and their students who struggle to envision a Christian religious education adequate for the challenges of forming personal and congregational faith in our contemporary world.

The second includes laity in the church: those seeking to understand the adaptive challenges they are facing in their congregations' educational ministries, as well as parents seeking support from their congregations for the nurture of the faith of their children.

Those responsible for faith forming education in evangelical Protestant, Roman Catholic, and Orthodox religious traditions make up a third audience for the discussion that follows. They may find in it parallels to their own experience of the adaptive challenges they face in forming the faith of their children and youth.

A fourth group includes social scientists, historians, theological educators, and educational theorists interested in the larger conversation about the changing place and role of religion and education in American society. Much has been written about changes in the religious and spiritual culture of the nation and their impact on congregations and their denominations. Little has been written about the response of those church bodies and their leaders to those changes. Hence my attention focuses on the unintended as well as the intentional complicity of those denominations in the changes that have had such an impact on the role and place of children and youth in their congregations.

I hope the discussion that follows will reinvigorate conversations about the function and role of education in forming identity, shaping character, and cultivating practices that deepen and sustain the faith of persons while revitalizing, at the same time, their traditions of belief and practice. Early in the nineteenth century, during another era of significant upheaval in the nation and much confusion in the churches about how to influence the future of the faith of their children, Horace Bushnell,[20] a prominent pastor at the time, pointed out the problem I seek to address. When a community does not educate its young, he observed, it must find youth and adult converts to its way of life if it is to survive beyond the present generation. That has been the most serious flaw in the strategies of the *church renewal movement* of the 1960s and 1970s and the more contemporary *church growth* and *emerging church* movements. None of these movements has addressed the dual challenge of maintaining while renewing the faith of congregations from one generation to the next. They have not focused attention on the interdependent challenges of nurturing in children and youth a life of faith while handing on and renewing through them their traditions of faith for the new circumstances and situations in which they will find themselves.

I therefore envision this work as a wake-up call to leaders in the congregations of the old Protestant mainline, their denominations, and the schools that train their clergy. I want to encourage constructive thought that moves beyond the immediate concerns of congregational life to the challenges of being viable communities of faith through successive generations both for the sake of their faith traditions and the vitality of the faith of the children and youth who participate in them.

Overview

I have organized the discussion that follows into five chapters. The first takes up the task of thinking in a general way about education in forming faith. Special attention is given to its aims, its function in congregations and communities, and the agencies most central to the challenges of forming personal and corporate faith for the times in which we live.

The second chapter focuses attention on what happened to education in the cultivation of the faith of children and youth in old mainline Protestant congregations in the midst of the changing cultural and religious landscape of the nation after World War II. This chapter begins with a case study of the responses in one denomination to the adaptive challenges it encountered in its education through these cultural shifts. Through this

---

20. Bushnell, *Christian Nurture*, 58–60.

discussion it is my intent to highlight sources to the adaptive challenge of education congregations now face in forming the faith of their children.

The third chapter takes up this adaptive challenge by focusing on the necessary interdependence of developmental, practice, and discovery learning in a faith-forming education and the task of recovering practice learning in the formation of the faith of a congregation's young people.

The fourth chapter explores the adaptive challenge of re-forming congregations as catechetical cultures. Attention will be focused on reclaiming congregational practices of hospitality, celebration, and conversation as crucial influences in congregational faith-forming education.

The re-forming of congregations as catechetical cultures does not happen by accident. It requires the exercise of an ecclesially grounded educational imagination adequate to the task of re-envisioning a congregation's future through the faith of its young people. The final chapter takes up the task of exploring the shape and agency of that imaginative capacity in congregations caught up in the contemporary dynamics of social, cultural, and religious pluralism, marketplace economics, and technological innovation. An ecclesial imagination in this situation, I will argue, requires that congregations must move beyond tinkering with existing pedagogies, producing new curriculum resources, or adapting existing programmatic agencies for teaching and learning. Instead they must dare to think in fresh ways about the constitutive features of a faith-forming education. Clues to those features already exist, I contend, in the exercise of the ecclesially grounded educational imaginations of congregations here and there, now and again across the country. These clues provide a road map for strategic conversations among church leaders to guide their quests for a future for their congregations through the faith of their children and youth.

Acknowledgements

I began working on this book shortly after my retirement from Candler School of Theology in 2000. An opportunity to direct the Carnegie Foundation for the Advancement of Teaching study of clergy education intervened and I did not return to the manuscript until late in 2007. By that time my thinking about what I needed to do had changed significantly. My original intent had been primarily to tell the story of what had happened to the educational vision and strategies of the denominations often described now as the old Protestant mainline. That effort, with the encouragement of

Duane Ewers and Judy Smith, long-time colleagues associated with United Methodist educational and publishing agencies, became the original version of chapter two. Conversations with colleagues during the Carnegie Foundation study of clergy education and a judicatory task force on leadership led me to conclude this was not enough. I also needed to think constructively, about what an education of faith formation might look like for the future. The result of that effort is found in the pages that follow.

Although I bear responsibility for the content of this work, I have had many conversation partners along the way whose questions, stories, and insights have significantly influenced my thinking. An earlier version of the discussion in chapter three was included in a set of essays edited by James Michael Lee called *Forging a Better Religious Education in the Third Millennium*.[21] An invitation from James Lewis to give a lecture at the Louisville Institute provided the impetus to some of chapters four and five. Through the years I have explored many themes that found their way into the discussion that follows in seminary class sessions, local church workshops, conversations with graduate students and colleagues in the field, as well as in academic and church conference lectures.

More immediate partners in the project have included the ministry staff and Christian education committee members of the congregation my wife and I attend. Dan Pitney, Robin Morrison, Roberta Moore, Kristen Bonn, Sharon Everette, Ann Shaffer, Nancy Porter, and Shannon Riggs graciously read and gave feedback on various parts of the manuscript. Jeanne Carley, Ethel Johnson, Mary Lou Reddig, Paul Henshaw, and Jerome Hamm, as insiders to stories I tell throughout the book, reviewed them to confirm their authenticity.

I am indebted to Sue Detterman for her research into the parallel story of what happened to the agencies of Christian education in her own United Church of Christ mainline Protestant denomination. I have relied on the feedback and suggestions of several people who read the chapters as they were being written, especially Sue Detterman and Joe Hoffman, both former students in my classes and now pastors of United Church of Christ congregations. Dale Otto, a retired professor who studies the language development of children, helped me clarify ways of thinking about the relationship of practice and developmental learning. A continuing correspondence with Douglas Purnell, artist, pastor, and pastoral theologian in Sidney, Australia,

---

21. Foster, "Why Don't They Remember? Reflections on the Future of Congregational Education," 89–112.

about each of the chapters has been a primary source of inspiration and wise counsel. He has been especially helpful in describing similarities in the adaptive challenges facing American U.S. and Australian mainline Protestant church education. I am indebted to Dorothy Bass, Joyce Mercer, and Jack Seymour for reviewing the full draft of a penultimate version of the manuscript. Their generous comments and perceptive insights significantly clarified and sharpened what I was trying to say.

Janet Foster, my wife and colleague of many years, read every word several times with a special eye for awkward phrases, confusing statements, and unclear arguments. No words can adequately express my appreciation for her love and support throughout the whole writing process. For the support and encouragement of each of these persons throughout the project, I am deeply grateful.

Discussion Questions and Exercises for Personal and Group Reflection

Following each chapter you will find questions and exercises designed to explore themes from the chapter more fully. They may prompt personal reflection and study. They can be a springboard for group discussion in congregations and classrooms or with groups of clergy and religious educators. They may suggest other questions. Choose those that seem most relevant to your situation.

1. Have you heard variations on the lament of the women at the beginning of this chapter? If so, what seemed to be the primary concerns you have heard?

2. How would you describe the differences between a technical and an adaptive challenge?

3. In what ways does the lament at the beginning of the chapter pose both a theological and an educational adaptive challenge?

4. What evidence do you see that members in the congregation you know best envision a future for themselves through the faith of their children and youth?

5. Would you like to explore issues introduced in this chapter more deeply? If so, one way to do so is to interview someone who taught

or led children or youth in a congregation before 1970 and someone currently teaching in that same congregation today. Ask these persons

a. How were they recruited?

b. What kind of training and support did they receive?

c. How would they describe the purposes for student learning in the curriculum resources they were using?

d. What were their personal goals for student learning?

e. Then compare and contrast their perceptions of their experiences. In what ways do their comments highlight challenges your congregation faces in cultivating the faith of its children and youth?

Chapter One

Education in Forming Faith

Let's say that when I was a little baby, and all my bones soft and malleable, I was put in a small Episcopal cruciform box and so took my shape. Then, when I broke out of the box, the way a baby chick escapes an egg, is it strange that I had the shape of a cross?

—JOHN STEINBECK, *The Winter of Our Discontent*

Introduction

Themes in this chapter are rooted in an assumption I bring to any discussion of education. We are relational creatures. This assumption also grounds the Christian life. We are loved by God. In turn we are to love God with our whole being and our neighbors as ourselves. That is the basic structure of the covenants of Abraham and Moses that bound our ancestors and still binds us in relationship to God and each other. The implication, as the writer of the letter to the Ephesians suggests in his vision of the church, is to live as "members one of another."[1] The consequence is that even if we try to separate ourselves from any contact with others, we still know ourselves primarily in relation to the others from whom we have distanced ourselves.

1. Eph 5:25.

I build on this assumption to explore a way of thinking about education, particularly the education of congregations in forming (which includes transforming) Christian faith and practice. This discussion establishes a framework through which I will then seek in the next chapter to explain why the old Protestant mainline denominations after the 1960s abandoned education as a means of assuring their own futures. In subsequent chapters, I will then explore clues to the adaptive challenge this action created for their contemporary congregations.

The Impulse in Communities to Educate

In *The Creative Word*, Old Testament professor Walter Brueggemann explores sources to the persistence of Jewish community identity through many centuries. He wonders why the children of Abraham and Sarah could survive repeated experiences of war, exile, and persecution. He concludes their continuing viability as a community could be traced to a persevering commitment to education.[2] An early description of that commitment is found in the sermon Moses delivered as the Israelites prepared to cross the Jordan River into the long awaited Promised Land. Its key elements, found in the sixth chapter of the book of Deuteronomy, not only continue to influence contemporary Jewish life and practice: they speak to the current situation of Christian congregations as well.

The impetus to education for the writer of this ancient sermon originated in the desire of the Israelite tribes "that all would go well" for them in this new land "flowing with milk and honey" so they might "multiply greatly."[3] The inference, of course, was to their desire to become a great nation. The sermon did not outline a military, political, or economic strategy for the realization of that dream. Instead, Brueggemann argues that it emphasizes a subtle and radical insight about community and nation building; namely that any community wanting "to last beyond a single generation must concern itself with education."[4] His insight, I contend in the pages that follow, is as true for contemporary congregations and their denominational traditions as it was for a confederation of Hebrew tribes several thousand years ago. That means we need to be clear about what we mean by education.

2. Brueggemann, *The Creative Word*, 1.

3. Deut 6:3.

4. Brueggemann, *The Creative Word*, 1.

Since the distinctive feature of the ancient community of Israel was its relationship to God, its education necessarily centered on learning to obey the commandment to "love the Lord your God with all your heart, and with all your soul, and with all your might."[5] The practice of obedience could not be assumed or left to chance. It had to be cultivated through intentional effort. About what that effort might entail, the sermon is quite specific. If the Israelites were to succeed in this adventure of community building, they needed to keep the words of the commandments in their hearts. They could do this by:

- Reciting them to their children;

- Talking about them at home and away from home;

- Wearing signs of the commandment on their hands and emblems of their bond to God on their foreheads;

- Posting them on the doorposts of their homes;

- Exercising the commandments, decrees, and statutes of God in their relationships with their neighbors and the activities of daily life;

- And telling the stories of God's liberating activity to answer their children's questions about why they had to do these things.[6]

These ancient instructions suggest a way of thinking about education still relevant in our own time. They distinguish its outcomes for learning, for instance, from the processes of enculturation that are the object of anthropological study and those of socialization explored by sociologists. The difference, as historian Lawrence Cremin emphasizes, is that families, congregations, communities, and nations through education intentionally seek to "transmit or evoke" the "knowledge, attitudes, values, skills, and sensibilities" deemed central to the continuing vitality of their identity and character.[7] Again this does not happen by chance. It involves *deliberate* decisions about what needs to be learned, how, when, and where. It establishes *systematic* patterns of teaching and learning for increasingly complex ways of knowing, doing, and being. It is embedded in a web of agencies that *sustain* and *reinforce* these patterns of teaching and learning from one generation into the next.[8] These terms highlight the purposefulness of

---

5. Deut 6:4.

6. Deut 6:7–10, 17–18, 20–25.

7. Cremin, *American Education*, xiii.

8. Ibid.

education, but they do not yet clarify what it does. Again in the sermon of Moses we may find clues to its distinguishing features. I focus attention on three: its function, aims, and agencies.

The Function of Education

Brueggemann identifies two functions of education pertinent to our discussion. In the first, education is concerned with *maintaining* the identity and character, practices and traditions of a community over time in and through those who identify with them. Through education a community discerns a course for its future in the resources of its heritage.[9] This is as true for congregations and their denominational traditions as it was for ancient Israel. Each needs "enough continuity of vision, value, and perception"[10] to link the generations. This means the future of a community's identity depends significantly on the extent to which successive generations identify with the traditions, values, and practices they receive even as they, in turn, renew and hand them on to the generations that follow.

In congregations and their denominational traditions, however, the practices of forming faith in one generation for the sake of the generations that follow are not enough to ensure their long term future. A second function of education is also required. If the faith of a congregation and its members is to be *relevant* to the challenges of ever changing situations and always new circumstances, its education requires "enough freedom and novelty"[11] to survive in and be pertinent to the impact of those challenges on their future. This suggests that the maintenance of congregational identity, character, and practice can only be sustained if it is renewed through the regeneration of the faith of its members in each passing generation. Forming faith in congregations can only be renewed, consequently, as it is also transformed.

This insight I encountered most clearly in Robert MacAfee Brown's discussion of the dynamics at work in the practice of faith.[12] Brown seeks to understand how faith shapes our identities and forms our commitments. As he probes how faith works, he observes it has to do with something that happened in the past that we must "put to some use." This insight may be

---

9. Brueggemann, *The Creative Word*, 1.
10. Ibid.
11. Ibid.
12. Brown, *Is Faith Obsolete?*, 25–36.

stated another way: something happened in the past that makes a claim on us that we must somehow acknowledge and engage. He notes we typically associate that "something" with a past event through which we begin to understand who we are and what we are to do with our lives. For all of us an important event influencing how we understand ourselves is the occasion of our births. It makes a difference whether we were born during the depression or the Vietnam War or after 9/11 because each event distinctively shapes the conditions through which we form our perceptions of and responses to the challenges we face daily.

For the followers of Moses, that event in the past was the liberating activity of God freeing them from the oppression of slavery, leading them through the chastening experience of the wilderness, and bringing them into the Promised Land. For most Americans, that event was the establishment of a new community, indeed, a new nation, freed from dominating religious and political institutions. For Christians, that event (or more properly, cluster of events) is centered on Jesus of Nazareth. His life, death, and resurrection establish both the purpose and shape of our lives as his followers. That event did not just happen in the distant past. The trajectory of its influence and meaning continues into the present and future as we participate in and extend its traditions and practices embedded in the histories of Catholic, Orthodox, Reformed, Wesleyan, or Pentecostal communities of faith.

Brown describes the mutuality of transmitting and renewing, forming and transforming faith as the "creative appropriation" of a past that becomes increasingly "open" as we come to know more about it.[13] In other words, the practice of faith from this perspective is an inherently educational practice. It relies on continued learning not only in the experience of each of us but also in the experience of our communities and congregations. It emphasizes the mutuality of a community's quest to *form* in each successive generation values, commitments, and practices integral to its identity and the *transformation* of those same values, commitments, and practices in response to our encounters with the redemptive activity of God in our midst.

This is not such a strange insight. We can see this pattern of engagement in our own responses to the stories we have heard about the Christ event. We may have first heard stories of that event as children. Through the years we may have heard those stories many times. At some point a

13. Ibid., 28–29.

story or group of stories attracts our attention. We read them again and again. We find ourselves thinking about them at odd times of the day. We begin to anticipate the repetition of their increasingly familiar storylines. We ponder what they might be saying to us; how they may be influencing our thinking or our relationships with others. They begin to shape our perceptions and actions. We begin to be more attentive to strangers. We make more frequent and larger contributions to the community food bank. We may discover in our prayers renewed energy and focus. At some point we may find ourselves making a change in the way we prioritize our time and resources. We may not recognize how the content of those stories is beginning to shape what we think and how we act, but as they become increasingly important to us we may find ourselves caught up in acts of *creatively appropriating*; i.e., internalizing and embodying perspectives, values, and commitments embedded in them. Education in the formation of Christian identity and practice, consequently, is an inherently theological practice. Originating in the human quest to discern, relate to, and understand God, its theological shape is nowhere more evident than in its aims.

The Aims of Education

If the function of education is to ensure the maintenance and renewal of a community through the present and into the future, then its aim or task in Christian communities is to facilitate the learning that fosters faith in the creative and redemptive work of God. The issue is not learning for its own sake, but the learning that cultivates the vitality of the relationship of congregations and their members to the God who calls them into community. We do not have to be taught to learn. From birth we begin to exert our curiosity. We give expression to desires and longings that expand our worlds. We seek connections with purposes and meanings that exceed our understanding. We struggle to make sense of the consequences of our personal and collective actions. Our capacities for self-transcendence lead us to anticipate the mystery associated with the word "God." Our growing bodies and developing minds provide the impetus for ever new opportunities of learning. To be human is to learn. To learn, in turn, is an adventure of faith. We do not know nor can we fully anticipate the outcomes of our learning.

The learning required for the continuing vitality of the faith of a community or congregation in the creative and redemptive work of God, however, cannot be left to chance. It must be cultivated if its integrity is to persist from one generation to the next. That ancient sermon of Moses to the Israelites highlights three modes of learning relevant to our discussion of education in forming faith. Each emphasizes a different impetus to and readiness for learning in each of us. At the same time each evokes a different responsiveness on the part of the educating community for our learning. And yet, they are necessarily interdependent in the mutuality of forming and transforming personal and community faith. These three modes of learning may be described as *developmental learning, practice learning*, and *discovery learning*.

Developmental learning. During the last half-century and more a number of scholars and researchers directed our attention to the patterns of *developmental learning*. Each focuses their attention on some cluster of "developmental learning tasks" in the human experience. Among the more prominent of these researchers, Erik Erikson explores the development of our ego-identities, Jean Piaget our cognitive development, Lawrence Kohlberg our moral development, and James Fowler our faith development. Their insights have since been refined and tweaked in many ways by subsequent generations of scholars. Their basic shared insight, however, dominates my attention; namely, that in adulthood we may discern the goal of our learning from infancy on. In the faithfulness of adults we may discover models for the faithfulness of children and youth. What we learn as infants, consequently, become building blocks for our learning as younger and then older children. What and how we learn as adolescents gathers up and transforms what and how we learned as children. This pattern of learning continues into and through adulthood. Our learning, in other words, is neither simply linear nor neatly sequential. Erikson illustrates this accumulative process with a wonderful image related to the subject of his own research. In a child's development, "a lasting ego-identity . . . cannot be completed without a promise of fulfillment" in adulthood. As a child grows that promise "reaches down" into the "baby's beginnings" to cultivate "an accruing sense of ego strength."[14] In terms of our discussion, this has to do with claiming the influence of our growing consciousness of our relationship to God in our lives. This happens most effectively, Erikson adds, when the context of our learning is a healthy one. His observation is crucial to this discussion.

We can see Erikson's insight in the rudiments of our own adult experience in our experience as children. For example, when I was a young child the stories, images, and sounds associated with the promise of faith I encountered in adults reading the Bible washed over me in worship services

14. Erikson, *Childhood and Society*, 218.

(since my mother did not believe in church nurseries for children) and during family devotions. As I grew older I began to distinguish one story from another while listening to my parents and Sunday school teachers tell them. I developed favorites among them. I wanted them to hear them over and again. In second grade my parents gave me a book of Bible stories. I now had the opportunity to read the stories on my own. The stories of the Old Testament especially caught my imagination. I returned to them repeatedly. Some found their way into my play, as I imagined myself with David facing Goliath or with Joseph as his brothers sold him into slavery. My elementary Sunday school teachers created activities through which those stories often came alive. I especially remember a summer Vacation Bible School in which they helped us build an elaborate Palestinian village in which we dramatized stories of Jesus we had been studying.

Somewhere during junior high I began to ask increasingly difficult questions about those stories. Why did the Bible contain two creation stories? Why did God favor Abel? Why would a loving God destroy everyone and everything in the world with the exception of one family? And even more perplexing, how did Noah keep all those animals alive on that ark? My high school Sunday school teacher was ready for me and my peers. He encouraged our questions. I am now aware he also posed questions to push us to ask even more challenging questions. That class helped prepare me for the rigorous critique of biblical literature in college courses on the Old and New Testaments. There I began to explore in a disciplined fashion the origins and meanings of biblical texts. More profoundly, each of these moments of learning depended on my previous learning even as they also prepared me for the next.

As I reflect back on my experience of encountering and engaging the Bible my attention is drawn to two clues for the cultivation of developmental learning among children, youth, and adults in the maintenance and renewal of faith in congregational life. The first has to do with the role of the culture of the congregation as a catechetical context for my learning. It can be stated this way: a congregation's engagement with the stories of Jesus and the experience of biblical peoples with God creates an environment either supporting and reinforcing or hindering and diminishing the changing interest and engagement of its members with those same stories from childhood into adulthood. That is the point in Moses' sermon in which the Israelites are urged to recite the commandment daily. This practice had the potential of creating a context of encouragement for the questions of children. I am now aware that as a child I simply assumed the Bible was central to the faith of my family and congregation. We read and studied it. Its images and stories filtered through the conversations I heard. It inspired difficult questions, often posed by my father, that were not brushed aside, but instead taken seriously. The culture of my family and church, in other words, encouraged any interest I might have had in exploring the stories of Jesus.

The second observation is closely related. When a congregation's children, youth, or adults give evidence of some new level of engagement with the faith of the community, their faith is nurtured more clearly in congregations that embrace their readiness to ask new and reformulated questions and to pose new concerns. In Moses' sermon this readiness to respond to the initiative of the learner is highlighted in the expectation that adults are to take seriously the questions of children. It was evident in my own experience as my questions for information shifted to questions for meaning and purpose.

Anticipating the developmental shifts in the learning of children and youth has for years been a major theme in the preparation of curriculum resources in the denominations of the old Protestant mainline denominations. In the nineteenth century, curriculum producers first began to publish resources designed specifically for children, youth, and adults. During the mid-twentieth century curriculum resource writers and editors published curriculum resources with explicitly developmental categories in mind. Age appropriate learning goals were deliberately identified. Curricular units were systematically ordered to lead children and youth through progressively more complex encounters with the objects of their learning. The intention in this widely acclaimed and ecumenical approach to curriculum[15] was to anticipate the learning children and youth would bring to their Sunday school classes as they moved from one stage of development to the next. Most contemporary curriculum resources continue to support and reinforce developmental learning. Missing in them, however, is much attention to a second mode of learning integral to any education concerned with the formation of faith.

This complementary aim of education may be described as the cultivation of *practice learning. Practice learning is directed to the competency of our participation in the community or communities with which we identify.* The impetus to practice learning originates in the mutuality of our personal

15. The ecumenical commitment to the importance of developmental theories in understanding the learning of children, youth, and adults culminated in The Cooperative Curriculum Project of the National Council of Churches, published as *The Church's Educational Ministry: A Curriculum Plan.*

desire to belong and be taken seriously by some community with which we might identify and the community's desire to envision a lively and robust future through us. Practice learning emphasizes the quest for effective and competent participation. We can see the impulse to practice learning in children who imitate the models of behavior and attitude of an older sibling or the members of a peer group. It can be seen in the child who accepts the coaching of a parent or teacher through the repetitions of some progressively more complex learning task.

The significance of practice learning for a community of faith is highlighted in the sermon of Moses as he encourages the Israelites to recite the commandments over and again and to talk about them at home and away from home. Through the repetitions of practice the words move beyond familiarity to shaping perceptions and actions; to establishing a standard for personal participation in the life of the community. Learning is consequently embodied. It gives form to the relationship of the words we are "learning" to our interactions with others and the events and circumstances of our daily experience. As people talk about these words with others they participate in conversations with the potential to deepen both their understandings of the words and the claim they have on the lives of those who speak them. As children first overhear these conversations and then begin to imitate and expand on them, their own faith practice attunes them to the nuances of the rhythms, themes, and patterns of interaction embedded in them. As they repeat the practice over and over again they begin to develop the confidence for ever more competent participation in the community of these conversations. An outcome of their practice may well be the intensification of their identification with each other, their heritage and future together; indeed, with God, as the ultimate object of their learning.

The notion of practice learning is familiar to us as we think about how we learn to play a musical instrument or game, hone a skill through its repetition, or become proficient in a new language. We often pay less attention to the importance of practice learning in cultivating some new level of excellence in our worship and mission, our leadership or care for each other. We have high expectations of a surgeon and of the drivers we meet on the road. Our expectations of the excellence in the practices of our faith should be no less high. Practice learning, in this sense, is directed toward some standard of excellence. It can be as explicit as gathering a group of children into the rehearsal of a song of faith until its words, melody, and rhythms are so embedded in their memories and bodies they can sing it for a special occasion unselfconsciously and with the freedom that only comes from robust knowing. It can be as complex as learning to participate in a liturgical or missional practice with the spontaneity that only occurs in deep and intimate knowing. Again a personal example of my learning to participate in the practice of faith may illustrate my point.

Methodists have historically been a singing people. Charles and John Wesley, founders of the Methodist movement in the eighteenth century, wrote hundreds of hymns. Many can still be found in contemporary hymn books. As I was growing up I experienced a fairly strong expectation that belonging to a congregation in that tradition involved learning to participate in its singing. I encountered that expectation in my family. It may sound old fashioned now, but my mother sang hymns while she worked around the house. Every so often my father would persuade us to gather around the piano for a family song fest that included favorite hymns. That expectation was expanded in the public schools I attended. I memorized more Christmas carols through grade school for the annual school Christmas pageant than I did in church. Throughout high school I either accompanied on the piano or joined the choir in singing the Christmas portion of Handel's *Messiah*.

My musical vocabulary of faith, however, was most explicitly cultivated in church. All ages sang hymns and gospel tunes together during the weekly Sunday school assembly. We sang many of the same hymns during monthly potluck suppers. We sang hymns during worship. As I look back on those years I realized the congregation had a core curriculum of hymns. We sang many songs and hymns so often I could eventually sing some of them from memory—beginning as a small child with "Jesus Loves Me, This I Know" and continuing through grade school with hymns ranging from "Holy, Holy, Holy," to "The Old Rugged Cross," to "Tell Me the Stories of Jesus," and my father's favorite, "In the Garden." The practice of hymns intensified during my adolescence. A part of each Sunday evening youth group meeting was devoted to singing a wide variety of camp songs, gospel choruses, and hymns. Sub-district rallies of youth from several congregations always began with the singing of choruses as a warm-up for the singing of hymns. My hymn repertoire expanded. "Be Thou My Vision," "Are Ye Able," "Make Me a Captive Lord," "O For a Thousand Tongues to Sing," "The Church's One Foundation," along with the carols of Christmas and the hymns of Easter, became part of my faith vocabulary. Those local events of singing with other youth were replicated on a larger scale in regional and national conferences and convocations and especially during summer camp. During that week we practiced hymns for daily worship. We studied the texts of hymns that reinforced the study theme for the week. We practiced singing the hymns as sopranos, altos, tenors, and basses. And some hymns so moved us that upon our return home we urged our congregations to sing them.

Through the practice of hymn singing, in other words, I participated in a common practice in my denominational tradition of forming faith. As one who enjoyed music in the first place and was surrounded by music in the second, it was a practice with which I obviously identified. As I grew older I realized I was articulating many of my deepest faith convictions in the words of hymns I knew. Singing "God of Grace and God of Glory," I encountered the outpouring of God's power. When singing "At the Name of Jesus Every Knee Shall Bow," I discovered myself in the company of the congregation in Philippi exhilarated over receiving and reading a letter from the apostle Paul. The singing of hymns continues to be one of the highlights of congregational worship for me. In the singing of hymns I often sense myself most clearly in the presence of God. This, however, is only one small practice in a Christian congregation. Practice learning is equally as crucial in reading the Bible, conversing about beliefs and doctrines, giving leadership to committees, offering prayers of intercession, caring for the sick, feeding the homeless, visiting the imprisoned, and strategizing ways to address some social, economic, or political issue in the local community or many miles away. It takes practice to participate in any of them effectively.

Discovery learning necessarily complements developmental and practice learning in congregations seeking to maintain and renew the faith of their ancestors through the education of their children. Through discovery learning we begin to *imagine new possibilities for living faithfully in our always new situations and ever changing circumstances.* In the instructions of Moses, we see a common catalyst to discovery learning in the questions of children. Their curiosity pushes at the boundaries of our knowing, doing, and being. It is the impetus to the exploration of new possibilities in our interpretations of old stories, the springboard to new insights, the catalyst to yet-to-be explored lines of investigation or inquiry. It leads to the revelation of alternatives we had not previously taken seriously. It is an important catalyst to hope.

Discovery learning is often associated with the theories of John Dewey. He had observed that the disposition in children toward exploration and discovery was a powerful precondition to continued learning. As adults we typically enjoy the exercise of a child's imagination and curiosity. We typically encourage young children to probe the worlds around them. We are intrigued by their experiments in articulating theological ideas and their imaginative wording of prayers. We are often less enthusiastic about the impulse to discovery learning among older children, teenagers, and curious adults because their questions often push us to address lines of inquiry we had not previously considered. They may urge us to examine something we have previously resisted or rejected. They may reveal our ignorance about something or draw attention to the limits of our skills. Discovery learning, however, is a critical source for the maintenance and renewal of congregational life, because it explicitly engages us in the "creative" appropriation of our faith traditions to address the disruptions of our changing social and historical contexts. Discovery learning is the mode of learning that draws us most closely into the mystery of God.

When I think about how discovery learning facilitates the task of maintaining and renewing congregational life I am reminded of a group of seventh-, eighth-, and ninth-grade youth with whom I worked several years ago. The seventh graders were currently in a confirmation class. The older youth had been confirmed during the previous two years. As we were brainstorming ideas for the theme of our winter retreat one of the older youth asked a perfectly appropriate developmental learning question: "why do we believe what we do?" This prompted another youth to ask "where did we get our beliefs?" Their questions prompted a lively discussion about their struggles over what to believe from all the possibilities for believing they were encountering. Their questions caught the imagination of the rest of the group.

After several more weeks of planning the group decided to divide the youth attending the retreat into five different groups. Each assumed the role of being an early Christian congregation from places like Corinth, Ephesus, and Rome. Each of these congregations would receive a letter from a *bishop* describing first of all, how their differences in talking about their beliefs had become a general problem for all their congregations, and second, requesting that they send representatives to a council of churches to develop a common statement of faith they might all be able to affirm. It was decided to limit the focus of their discussion to affirmations about God, Jesus, and the Holy Spirit. This meant we had to prepare brief biblical and theological statements drawn from the theological traditions of the church for each of these three theological categories to serve as resources for their discussion. During the study time of the retreat the youth gathered in the congregations to which they had been assigned to engage in the practice of learning to work their way through those statements to identify theological themes they wanted their representatives to emphasize in the council. The discussion was intense. It continued into their free time for sledding in the snow, over meals, and delayed "lights out" at bedtime. Finally, however, each of their congregations had a statement to present and the council gathered with the rest of the group serving as observers. Representatives from each congregation presented their statements of faith and a rationale for what they had included in it.

Then began the deliberations over how to word a statement each congregation could affirm. By this time the discussion was no longer objective. The exercise was no longer a simulation. Instead the views and commitments of the youth in that room were now on the table and open to debate. Observers jumped into the deliberations. Discussions became passionate. Disagreements created tension. It took much longer than we had anticipated. Eventually, however, a relatively straightforward statement of faith emerged from the discussion that everyone present could affirm. After returning home they shared it with the administrative council of the church which voted to use the statement they had written as the affirmation of faith in worship the next month.

In this description of their experience we may see something of the shape of discovery learning and its connections to developmental and practice learning. Questions prompt inquiry, investigation, or research that draw learners into the deeper dimensions of the question itself. Emerging insights, skills, and/or attitudes from this effort transform prior knowledge, skills, or attitudes. Again Brown's understanding of the dynamics of faith is helpful. Discovery learning focuses attention on the *creative* appropriation and thereby, the transformation of faith through new claims on our thought and in our lives. In that process discovery learning confronts us with the necessity of making decisions about the depth and extent to which we will commit ourselves to those new claims. This suggests the cultivation of discovery learning is crucial to the renewal of personal and congregational faith.

The view of education I am proposing requires the interdependence of *developmental, practice, and discovery learning in forming personal and congregational faith.* Together they nurture the learning that enables the members of a congregation to claim "I *am* Christian"; to assert that I follow Jesus in the particularities of some Methodist, Presbyterian, or Baptist community of faith. We may catch a glimpse of the interdependence of these three modes of learning in Moses' sermon embedded in the commandment to love God with all our heart, mind, and soul. As the cornerstone of Israelite identity it is the unifying feature in the life of the Israelite community. For Christians that commandment is amplified by a second directed to loving our neighbors as ourselves. These are not choices. Instead they distinguish who we are as a community of faith. Such learning cannot be left to chance. It must be *deliberately* engaged and *systematically sustained* over time if this community is to be renewed through its children.

When St. Paul urged those first Christian communities to recognize that some among them were only ready for "milk" while others were ready for more "solid food,"[16] he highlights a distinctive characteristic of the interdependence of these three modes of learning. It is *developmental* in that we learn best that which we are most ready to learn. It is *cumulative* as when the learning of a two- or four-year-old becomes a building block and catalyst for subsequent learning as a three or five year old. It becomes *transformative,* when again as St. Paul suggests, it leads us beyond our childish understandings and abilities to focus our attention on a deeper, more expansive, more complex, more excellent knowing, being, or doing through which we have a clearer sense of our identity and practice as Christian. The cultivation of learning in maintaining and renewing the faith of congregations and their members, however, requires more than interested or dynamic teachers and leaders attentive to the learning patterns of children, youth, and/or adults. It involves a web of educating agencies.

The Agencies of Education

The attention of an educating community to the interdependence of these three modes of learning leads us to a third clue to a way of thinking about education. *Forming faith in the maintenance and renewal of any community, including congregations, requires an alliance of agencies devoted to cultivating the interdependence of developmental, practice, and discovery learning.* The often quoted African proverb highlights a distinctive feature in this claim: "It takes a village to educate a child." Reflecting on James Carse's observation that *longevity* is the feature that most distinguishes religions,[17] I realized that educating for faith in the villages of our congregations requires the whole range of a religious tradition's cultural resources, including its music, literature, architecture, rituals, commitments, and practices

16. 1 Cor 3:2.
17. Carse, *The Religious Case Against Belief,* 142.

to give it form and focus. That insight is also assumed in the instructions of Moses for Israelite education. It involved the family, tribe, and village, and ultimately the nation, along with its sacred stories, texts, rituals, the temple, and eventually its synagogues for handing on and entering into its faith traditions.

We often confine our view of education, however, to some form of weekday, Saturday or Sunday, public or parochial schooling. In his study of education in forming American society, historian Bernard Bailyn challenges the limits of this view.[18] The Puritans, he reminds us, assumed the interdependence of the family and church with the schools in the education of their children and youth. Educational historian Lawrence Cremin pushes Bailyn's point. In his massive study of the history of American education he traces the interdependence of family, church, and school as well as a host of voluntary societies, publications, and in the twentieth century, various forms of media, in the nation's education.[19] Robert Lynn, influenced by Cremin's research, explores more closely the mutuality of the Sunday and public schools in American Protestant church education.

Even in our congregations, moreover, education has not been confined to notions of schooling. Congregations sponsor Sunday schools, weekday Bible studies, vacation Bible schools, youth fellowships, catechism and parent training classes, conferences, camping programs, and retreats. The various denominations all publish magazines, books, tracts, and devotional guides for individual and family study. For much of the latter part of the nineteenth and much of the twentieth centuries these different educating agencies shared to a remarkable degree a common set of values and practices reinforced in the experience of children and youth as they moved from family, to church, to school, and eventually into such groups as the scouts and 4-H.

I experienced something of this cohesiveness of educational influence I have been calling a catechetical culture in my first pastoral appointment in 1963. As I took up my responsibilities as Minister of Education in an upstate New York congregation, I, along with the members of the congregation, assumed a symbiotic relationship between the educational efforts of the congregation, its families, and the public schools of the community. Each day for, example, children in the congregation I served began their

18. Bailyn, *Education in the Forming of American Society*, 15ff.

19. See Cremin, *The Genius of American Education*, for a general introduction to themes in his work.

school day with a prayer that had been prescribed by state officials. In many schools the daily recitation of the Pledge of Allegiance was accompanied by a reading from the "Protestant" and usually, King James Version of the Bible. In the church sanctuary the American flag was displayed with the Christian flag and national holidays were approached with reverence. In schools children memorized Christmas carols every winter for the annual Christmas concert. Protestant clergy presided over baccalaureate services preceding graduation exercises. We assumed, in other words, that the interdependence of the public school and a community's Protestant churches provided a coherent and cohesive educational ethos for nurturing individual piety and citizenship, denominational and national loyalty, and a shared national Christian ethic.

In that pastoral appointment I also assumed I was an agent of the educational mission of The Methodist Church in and through that congregation. I trained teachers in and beyond the congregation to use developmentally appropriate curriculum resources produced by the denomination to systematically engage children and youth with Christian tradition and practice from year to year. I facilitated planning meetings to develop local educational ministries congruent with the general plan for local church education developed by the Division of the Local Church of the denomination's national Board of Education. I worked with a group of laity to train youth to be leaders of the youth fellowship in the congregation's ministry and to link them with youth from other congregations of the denomination in judicatory rallies, retreats, and camps. The senior pastor and I collaborated to coordinate the movement of people between the congregation's education and its worship and mission. I worked with members of the church in creating workshops and retreats where families could intergenerationally explore issues and practices of faith together. I became a resource person beyond my congregation to other churches in the community and throughout the regional judicatory. And I went through denominational training programs to be certified as a trainer of teachers and leaders in youth ministry in regional and national workshops and laboratory schools and as a writer of curriculum resources for youth.

There is nothing necessarily ideal or exemplary about these configurations of educational influence. Only with time did we become aware of the religious, gender, racial, and class biases in the educational structures of the community and denomination with which I was associated. Those biases eventually contributed to their collapse, an issue we will explore more fully in the next chapter. Rather, what is important to see at this point in the interdependence of these educational institutions and processes is the reinforcing alignment of their influence in the learning of children and youth.

In the congregation I served, for example, parents taking their two-year-old to her Sunday school class in the church could anticipate something of her experience in that congregation over the course of her elementary and secondary school years. The cradle roll superintendent would have introduced them to Nancy Theodore, the lead teacher in a class for two-year-olds that took seriously their developmental capacities. They would get to know Shirley Neeley, Jeanne Carley, Carolyn Brittain, Kay Culver, and Grace Russell and other teachers their daughter would inevitably meet as she moved up through the grades. If they did not already know it, they would discover during regularly held parent meetings that these teachers had participated in workshops and lab schools conducted by denominationally certified leaders. They met quarterly together for further training and monthly in planning meetings for their teaching. And perhaps most important, most taught because they felt they had been called in some way to this ministry of teaching and learning. During those parent meetings they would be introduced to the design of the curriculum produced by the denomination and its structured sequence of developmentally appropriate encounters with stories of the Bible, beliefs of the church, and guidelines for the Christian life. They would also explore the role of the family in the nurture of a child's faith, share experiences of praying with their children, review Bible story books they might choose to use with their children, while exploring together challenges they faced in modeling Christian discipleship in their homes for their children. During family night events they would be introduced to practices linking worship and study in the congregation with that in the home.

If her parents were like most of their peers in that congregation they would have belonged to what the congregation called a "research group." These small groups of ten to twelve persons met at least bi-weekly to explore the challenges of a life of faith. They would probably have participated as well, in a lively Sunday morning adult education program of elective courses involving a sizeable segment of the congregation. These adult education options were not typically found in congregations of the old Protestant mainline during the early 1960s. Most congregations gathered successive groups of young adults into classes that would remain together into their old age. These groups usually relied on denominationally produced curriculum resources to develop a growing familiarity with the content of the

Bible. The adults in this congregation, however, had rejected this more traditional approach.

In this congregation this little girl would probably have begun participating regularly in the worship life of the congregation before she turned five. When she entered first grade she could join the youngest of the children's choirs and begin rehearsing ways to participate in congregational worship. Here she would learn some of the hymns of the church and during an expanded Wednesday afternoon session explore in greater depth some of the Bible stories she was encountering in the Sunday church school. Because the pastors visited the full range of Sunday school classes, taught in Vacation Church School, and may have been in their home, her parents would have assumed she would, like the older children in the church, view them as friends. Since they had been taking her to church fellowship dinners since she was a small baby, they would undoubtedly assume she knew people in the church of all ages and that many of her closest friends in the years ahead would be from church.

If they looked far enough ahead this family could anticipate that she would move on to the junior high class taught by Mrs. Steen and Mrs. Copp, the junior and then senior high youth fellowships mentored by Mr. and Mrs. Hester and Dr. and Mrs. Stuckey with their mission projects, retreats, study, and extensive involvement in district and conference youth activities and camping programs. They might even have been aware that the Student Secretary of the Women's Society of Christian Service would be sending her name to the college chaplain or Wesley Foundation Director of her college so that she could be invited into its campus ministry. Contacts with denominational college professors of religion during summer church camps might have influenced her decision to attend a denominational college or university. There she might have discovered still more possibilities for engaging the life of faith in denominationally sponsored conferences emphasizing study and prayer, mission trips, and "caravans" of students traveling across the country to help congregations with limited resources deepen and extend their ministries.

The formal educational structures of this congregation were more elaborate than those found in many congregations. Most congregations did not have a full-time Christian educator and many lacked the resources and sustained commitment of teachers this congregation enjoyed. At the same time, I grew up in a congregation of less than one hundred and fifty members with dedicated volunteer teachers using denominationally approved resources who had been trained for their tasks in judicatory workshops and lab schools. During the 1960s and 1970s I often taught teachers from small congregations with limited resources in workshops and lab schools. The educational ministries in these limited resource congregations shared many of the strengths of the congregation I served. Many men and women teaching or serving in these congregations as adult leaders in *youth work* (as it was often then called), viewed it at least as an avocation. They had been effectively and extensively trained for their roles in denominationally sponsored workshops and lab schools. Many laity from these congregations served as educational resource persons to other congregations. Denominational curriculum resources provided a systematic and widely shared introduction to its theological traditions and discipleship practices for children, youth, and adults. The interlocking network of congregation, judicatory, and national church educational agencies of the denomination generally sustained, in other words, the educational efforts in each agency.

There is nothing sacred about this particular set of interlocking influences in the education of the faith of this or any other two-year-old child. If one attended the Baptist, Episcopal, Presbyterian, and Catholic churches down the street from that congregation, one would have discovered some similarities and some differences in both the goals and structures of their education. More important is the extent to which one would discover they shared a common intent for their education to facilitate the eventual identification of their children with their traditions of faith. In a sense novelist Ferrol Sams' Southern Baptist image of being "raised right" is an appropriate one here as well.[20] For those in this Methodist congregation, Methodist traditions of being "raised right" did not emphasize assenting to propositions of doctrinal truth. Rather they emphasized learning to live into the distinctive practices of piety associated with being "Methodist" followers of Jesus Christ with others. The fullness of a child's experience of "church" in this view of education, in other words, encompassed the congregation's catechetical culture of teachings, relationships, ritual events, and moral guidance permeating the enabling structures for learning in the congregation, its families, and the denominational ties that supported them.

---

20. Ferrol Sams tells the story of the challenges to being "raised right" experienced by a Southern Baptist boy in college in *The Whisper of the River*. Sams' description of the confluence of parental, church, and community guidance characterized my own experience as a Methodist boy growing up in a Methodist congregation in the relatively unchurched Pacific Northwest.

The Rest of the Story

By 1980, in the congregation I once served, parents taking their two-year-old to the Sunday school would have had to make quite different assumptions about her education in faith.[21] Mainline Protestant congregations had generally lost both their privileges and place in American culture. Their denominations had responded to the changes they were experiencing by realigning their ministries and restructuring their bureaucratic institutions. The impact on congregations was almost immediate. Following new denominational guidelines for distributing congregational leadership, most teachers with a deep commitment to teaching had been rotated out of their roles. Many of those who had been teaching had taken gainful employment in the expanding job market for women and no longer had the time for teaching they once had. In some congregations, patterns of rotation now moved teachers in and out of a class every quarter or month. Since the leadership training programs of the denomination had been effectively dismantled, few of these rotating teachers received any training. More and more teachers were using resources they had personally chosen at the local Christian bookstore or that had been chosen randomly from a display of optional curriculum resources at some judicatory conference.

Although congregations, especially those with professional leadership, often held on to a systematic view of what should be taught in classes for children, any coherence of teaching and learning from early childhood through adolescence and from one congregation in the denomination to the next had effectively disappeared. Randomness predominated among teachers, in curriculum, in educational settings, and in the experience of church life in general. Children's choirs, fellowship dinners, even mission and service projects had become programmatic options to be negotiated in the family calendar. Worship of children with the adults of the congregation had become even more elective than in the past. A few youth might be involved in the congregation's youth ministry. Most of those with an interest in matters of faith would have joined a para-church youth organization generally biased against denominational church tradition, adult authority, and theological inquiry. Still others would have dropped out of church altogether. More generally across the denomination of that congregation

21. The notion of a Church School to make visible the interdependence of all the educational activities of a congregation in Methodist Church Board of Education policy since the late 1940s all but disappeared. Once again a congregation's Christian education was increasingly identified with the *Sunday* school.

the numbers of local church, judicatory, and national staff members in Christian education had radically diminished. Denominational publishing houses had generally embraced a marketing, rather than an educational, strategy for the distribution of their resources. Even though some denominations experimented with early innovations in educational technology involving audio and video cassette tapes and television, they had little substantive impact on denominational education policies or programs. What happened? That story is the subject of the next chapter, but some comments related to the view of education developed in this chapter are relevant here.

After the 1960s the old mainline Protestant denominations generally abandoned education as a means to assuring their own futures. They had either forgotten or ignored the role of education in maintaining their distinctive faith traditions. This abandonment was most evident in the systematic dismantling of the web of educational agencies that sustained the interdependence of developmental, practice, and discovery learning in forming and transforming congregational faith and life. In the years that followed some Christian education leaders proposed creative alternatives to the thinking of congregations about their educational tasks. Their proposals, however, typically functioned as options in the religious education marketplace catching the attention of some local church leaders here and there for limited periods of time.[22] Denominational board and agency staff continued to develop new resources and strategies for revitalizing and renewing congregational identity and faith. Some of the most effective were directed to adults. The Lutheran's *Bethel Series* of Bible studies and The United Methodist's *Disciple: Becoming Disciples through Bible Study* have been among the most successful. Participants typically talk about how their faith is renewed and energized by their experience in them. These educational programs, however, have not become an integral part of some emerging web of agencies directed to maintaining the interdependence of developmental, practice, and discovery learning for all ages in forming congregational faith and identity.

Attention to developmental and discovery learning, consequently, tends, even in very large congregations that continue to attract large

---

22. Examples include the writings of John Westerhoff, *Will Our Children Have Faith?*; Jack Seymour, *Contemporary Approaches to Christian Education*; Jerome Berryman, *Godly Play*; Anne Streaty Wimberly, *Soul Stories;* and Richard Robert Osmer, *The Teaching Ministry of Congregations*. Each has been a catalyst to important conversations about education in forming faith in old mainstream Protestant denominations, but with generally limited impact.

numbers of children and youth, to be episodic. Learning activities may be developmentally appropriate and discovery learning activities may enrich the religious experience of children and youth, but they are not sustained long enough in practices that deepen or transform their developing faith. Congregations of the old Protestant mainline denominations, in other words, continue to sponsor many educational activities, but they lack the intentionality, the coherence, and the continuity needed to maintain and renew their identities as communities of faith. What happened to that catechetical culture in the congregations of the old mainline Protestant denominations? In the next chapter we begin to explore how an emphasis on technical rather than adaptive change helped undermine and subvert the educational efforts of their congregations in forming the faith of their children and youth.

Discussion Questions and Exercises for Personal and Group Reflection

1. In what ways might a congregation's education be a theological practice?

2. What contemporary challenges require us to think creatively about their appropriation by the children and youth in our churches to maintain the relevance of their faith through another generation?

3. Identify an important experience in your own faith education. In what ways did it contribute to your sense of the continuity of important values, ideas, or practices associated with the faith traditions of your denomination? To what extent did it engage you in the reinterpretation of those same values, ideas, or practices to ensure their continuing relevance for you?

4. In what ways might developmental, practice, and discovery learning each deepen and expand a child's theological understandings and faith commitments as they move from childhood into adolescence?

5. How would you describe the relationship of the influences of family, Sunday school, youth fellowship, congregational worship, congregational mission and/or service, and other settings both inside and outside the congregation in the formation of your own faith? Are those influences much the same for the children and youth you know?

6. Read one or more of the following books written by mainline Protestant Christian educators during the 1960s addressing the challenge of cultivating the faith of children and youth during a time of rapid social and religious change. You will probably have to request them from a seminary library through inter-library loan. Through your reading ask how the author thinks about the function, aims, and agency of the education in congregations in forming the faith of children and youth. Compare their views with those in this chapter.

Browning, R. L., *Communicating with Junior Highs* (Nashville: Graded Press, 1968).

Cully, Iris, *Children in the Church* (Philadelphia: Westminster Press, 1960).

Little, Sara, *Youth, World, and Church* (Richmond: John Knox, 1969).

Chapter Two

What Happened? An Adaptive Challenge!

It is a truism that Christian faith and education are inevitable compan-
ions. Wherever living faith exists, there is a community endeavoring
to know, understand, live, and witness to that faith. Still, an accurate
description of education in the church today is difficult. Here and there
exemplary educational ministries flourish, but in many more places
anxiety, confusion, frustration, despair, and even failure exist.

—JOHN H. WESTERHOFF III, *Will Our Children Have Faith?*

Introduction

Something happens most Sundays in the church we attend that has long intrigued me. One of the ministers invites children to the chancel area of the church. Three to five youngsters typically respond. Once in a great while, as many as ten to twelve children and at other times, no more than one or two come forward. When the latter happens, a couple of teenagers sitting nearby may join the group. They shuffle out of their pews with an amazing lack of self-consciousness. One Sunday when no children were present, several men took their place. Typically the children hear a story related to one of the scripture texts for the day, something about the current liturgical season, or some mission project of the congregation. This time together concludes with a prayer children and congregation repeat together line by line after the minister:

> *Dear God.*
> Dear God.
>
> *We thank you for this day.*
> We thank you for this day.
>
> . . . .
>
> . . . .
>
> *Amen!*
> Amen!

I only remember one pastor from my childhood who included a *sermon* for children in Sunday morning worship. It was not something we did in my early ministry even though most children in the congregation I served participated regularly in worship. Neither do I remember surrounding congregations engaging in the practice. Liturgical theologians did not promote or encourage the idea. At some point during the 1970s, however, most congregations in the area where we were living devoted a part of the liturgy to this instructional moment with children. I wondered why.

I was curious enough to explore the history of children's *sermons*. I discovered clergy had preached and published sermons for children in the nineteenth century, usually during special events for children and later in what came to be called "children's church." The addition of a children's sermon or "time for young people" to the weekly liturgy of a congregation has been a more recent innovation. Was it just a coincidence, I wondered, that its growing popularity coincided with the declining participation of children in the Sunday schools of old mainline Protestant congregations? In the congregation we attend children can participate in two different worship services. Fewer than forty preschool and elementary age children, however, are recorded on church rolls. That contrasts with more than ninety *preschool* children on the rolls of the slightly larger congregation I served back in the 1960s and the larger numbers of children in some of the more evangelical congregations in our community. Although families are smaller now, the real issue in our congregation is an aging membership. We do not have enough young families to ensure a lively and vital future for the congregation through their children. We are not alone. Hundreds of congregations across the country have fewer, even no children. If, as sociologist Wade Clark Roof suggests that "Children born into any faith community are the primary means by which that community replenishes itself," their absence creates a "serious problem" for their future.[1]

Pastors and Christian educators tell me children are "leaving church" at ever younger ages. Some leave, they say, due to competition from school, sports, and other community activities on Sunday morning, and others due to lack of parent commitment to their faith formation. That may help explain why the participation of children in the church we attend begins to decline after fourth grade. It does not explain what happens to the children who leave. It used to be assumed they would eventually return. Studies of young adults during this period of decline in mainline Protestant congregations, however, suggest this has not been the case for several decades.[2] They indicate that as many as two-thirds of contemporary young adults in church are not in a congregation of the denomination into which they were baptized or dedicated. Among those affiliated with a congregation, many "shopped" until they found one to fit their expectations of church. These expectations, however, were associated as often with television religion, non-denominational and para-church youth ministries, the generalized views of church in the culture, and the extravaganzas of popular concert culture as they were by the congregation of their childhood. Many others left the church never to return.[3] These studies reinforce my personal observation that congregations, especially those associated with the old mainline Protestant denominations, cannot assume in the twenty-first century

- the presence and participation of any child or youth;
- the continuing participation of children into adolescence;
- or the possibility that currently active youth will become as adults "faithful members" in some congregation of "Christ's holy church" or serve self-consciously as "Christ's representatives in the world."[4]

These reflections cause me to wonder if denominational identity is a thing of the past; if the "loyalty" people promise at confirmation or when they join the church may be confined to present involvement more than

1. Roof, *Spiritual Marketplace*, 51.

2. Scholars exploring this issue include among others, Dean R. Hoge and David A. Roozen, eds. *Understanding Church Growth and Decline*; Wade Clark Roof and William McKinney, *American Mainline Religion*; and Dean R. Hoge, Benton Johnson, and Donald A. Luidens, *Vanishing Boundaries*.

3. Roof, *Spiritual Marketplace*, 51–52; Cimino and Lattin, *Shopping for Faith*, ch. 4.

4. "Baptismal Covenant I," *The United Methodist Book of Worship*, 88.

to a way of living in a community of faith. They make me ask if the aging membership of many congregations will culminate in their inevitable demise. They lead me to question whether or not contemporary church leaders can find in their traditions of theology, liturgy, community life, and mission clues for living into a future they had not anticipated. My concerns are deeper than the institutional continuity of these congregations and their denominations. They have more to do with the continuing viability of their Reformation traditions to give form and substance to the faith of local communities of followers of Jesus into the unknown challenges that lie before us.

These questions bring me back to the observation that initially prompted me to write this book. During the 1960s and early 1970s the old Protestant mainline denominations generally abandoned education in the faith formation of their children and youth. There is nothing to indicate this was intentional. Church leaders had much on their minds. The social, economic, political, and religious landscape of the nation was in turmoil. As singer Bob Dylan declared in 1964, "The times," they were "a-changin." Civil rights movements disrupted long standing assumptions about the relationship of the races, men and women, gays and straights, old and young. Youth and young adult involvement in those movements and the protests against the Vietnam War challenged deeply ingrained notions of authority and leadership in the management of institutional life. Liberation movements in colonial societies confronted congregations with the paternalism of their missionary efforts. Technological innovations allied with a period of rapid global industrial expansion not only contributed to major population shifts among rural, urban, and suburban communities, they also created the conditions for major changes in the lifestyles of people. Immigrants introduced new but also ancient religious traditions into the religious fabric of the nation. Assumptions and practices in the education at the heart of congregational efforts to form the faith of their children and youth were being challenged from every side. As I look back on those years, leaders in congregations encountered four challenges that continue to hold my attention to this day:

- *the loss of reinforcing structures for their educational efforts.*

- *the loss of a catechetical culture of faith formation in congregations.*

- *the loss of a compelling narrative about God in the crosscurrents of theological, religious, and cultural diversity.*

- *the loss of intergenerational ties in mentoring faith formation.*

We have already noted that Ron Heifetz and Marty Linsky would call these *adaptive* rather than *technical challenges*.[5] They are particularly difficult because the loss of each cannot be retrieved. To move through or beyond those losses requires an "adaptive leap" of imagination to envision new or alternative solutions.[6] Many of the challenges facing the leaders of old mainline Protestant denominations back in the 1960s and 1970s were generally thought to be rooted in technical rather than adaptive problems. These leaders did not account for the impact of the losses associated with the changes they were experiencing. Those losses, however, continue to haunt the efforts of clergy and laity in forming the faith of their children and youth today.

The Loss of Reinforcing Structures

In the last chapter I described briefly how public schools had generally reinforced values and practices associated with the old mainline Protestant faith traditions into the 1960s. There was nothing particularly unusual about this relationship. Expectations for the interdependence of religion and education are deeply rooted in ancient Israel and the history of Christian societies. Historian Lawrence Cremin at Teachers College–Columbia University traced its more recent American pattern back to the middle of the nineteenth century, when "a generalized Protestant piety had become an integral part of the American vernacular, and the responsibility for teaching that piety to all Americans had become the central task of a newly constructed configuration of educative institutions"[7] involving the interdependence of families, schools, and churches. Across the street at Union Theological Seminary, Robert Lynn called the "partnership" of churches and schools in this configuration a "Protestant strategy of education."[8] In this strategic partnership, public schools promoted values of learning, piety, and civility identified with the civic traditions of Protestant Christianity, and congregations, primarily through their Sunday schools and auxiliary educational programs, taught children and youth the specifics of their own religious traditions. This partnership dominated the imaginations of

5. Heifitz and Linsky, *Leadership on the Line*, 13–14.

6. Ibid.

7. Cremin, *American Education*, 18.

8. For further discussion of how variations of this partnership worked for both Protestants and Catholics, see Jack L. Seymour, Robert O'Gorman, and Charles R. Foster, *The Church in the Education of the Public*, chs. 1–4.

Protestant church members across the country and was most influential in those communities where they most visibly dominated the local culture.

The seamlessness of this partnership in those communities may have been most visible in December as schools and churches prepared for the annual Christmas concert or pageant. As a child, for example, I joined the other children and youth in my congregation in rehearsing Christmas pageant story lines and roles and practicing carols and hymns for performances in congregational programs and Sunday school assemblies. At school in the weeks between Thanksgiving and the Christmas holidays, we rehearsed hymns, carols, readings, and skits during school hours for the annual Christmas program for the larger community. As a teenager I both accompanied on the piano and sang in the high school's annual presentation of the Christmas portion of Handel's *Messiah*. Should it be a surprise then, as a clergy friend suggested in the early 1980s, that at the time, the Christmas story was the one story from the Bible both church and non-church people knew best?

The influence of the partnership of Protestant church and public school was even more pervasive. The general piety of Protestantism generally influenced school assumptions about the character of the citizenship they were cultivating in their students, the values that informed the content of their textbooks, and their expectations of teacher attitudes and values. Many denominations in concert with the National Council of Churches dedicated resources and staff to the advocacy of public schooling and to interpreting challenges the churches and schools faced in educating the nation's children and youth. The general openness of mainline Protestant denominations to scientific insights created a relatively hospitable context for the schools to introduce new scientific discoveries into the teaching of history, science, and social studies. Perhaps the commitment to this partnership was most evident in the display of the American and Christian flags side by side in many predominantly white congregations.

During the 1960s and early 1970s this partnership collapsed in all but the most resistant communities, due significantly to pressure from groups it excluded or marginalized. These included long established Jewish communities, African Americans and other racial minorities, the increasing numbers of immigrants with different religious and cultural backgrounds, and those who rejected or did not identify with any religious tradition. Several court cases after World War II chipped away at the Protestant bias in the curriculum and practices of public education to make the culture of the schools more inclusive. Eventually the New York Supreme Court ban on formal sanctioned prayer in public schools, the U.S. Supreme Court ban on devotional reading in the schools, and a series of judicial and legislative decisions abolishing the racial segregation of schools dissolved the remaining remnants of the partnership. The collapse of this partnership undoubtedly hastened what Martin Marty called the dissolution and others have called the "dis-establishment" of the predominantly white old mainline Protestant denominations in the life of the nation.[9] The congregations of these denominations, consequently, not only lost their privileged place in the formation of American culture, they could no longer rely on public schools to reinforce their values and practices.

Many evangelical Protestant churches meanwhile refused to give up on the interdependence of family, school, and church in educating their children. The impact of their efforts may be seen today in at least two related movements. One is evident in their quite successful political advocacy for congenial religious perspectives in such things as the selection of public school textbooks.[10] The other can be seen among those who have given up on public schools for their own children and turned instead to privately funded schools or home schooling. In those settings they cultivate religious perspectives and moral values typically associated with evangelical Protestantism, promote visions and practices of family life based on a set of "biblical principles" articulated by persons and groups like James Dobson's *Focus on the Family*, and emphasize patriotism as a Christian responsibility.

Protestants of the old mainline denominations, in a contrary move, generally embraced greater cultural, racial, and religious diversity in the schools as a more accurate portrayal of the demographic reality of the nation with the affirmation that "each child is made in God's image" and thereby "deserves the best education available."[11] They took this to mean emphasizing "the importance of the separation of church and state, both for the churches and the schools," strengthening "support for public education in our faith communities," and encouraging the "active, appropriate involvement in public schools by congregations."[12] Advocacy, support, and

9. See for example, Marty, "The Establishment That Was," 1045; Hutchison, ed., *The Travail of the Protestant Establishment in America, 1900–1960*.

10. For example, much attention has been given by evangelical Protestants in Texas to the election of people with compatible views to the state Board of Education whose curriculum selections are adopted by schools in many other states across the nation.

11. From the most recent mission statement of the Committee on Public Education and Literacy of the Education and Leadership Ministries Commission posted on the National Council of Churches of Christ in the USA website, http://www.ncccusa.org.

12. Ibid.

the limitations that accompany notions of appropriate involvement, however, do not have the impact or influence that mutuality and interdependence once had on the mission and practices of either school or church.

In making this last claim I am not mourning the collapse. It had, in too many places and for too long, perpetuated and reinforced racial, religious, and class privilege and bias. Rather I share the general conviction held in most contemporary mainline Protestant denominations that a public school is truly public only if the full range of the religious, racial, linguistic, economic, and cultural diversity of children and their abilities are welcomed and embraced. My critique of denominational decisions in the midst of the collapse of the partnership of schools and churches centers instead, on their lack of imaginative attention to the impact of the losses of school reinforcement for the educational efforts of their congregations.

They viewed changes they were experiencing as technical rather than adaptive challenges. The consequences have been significant. They lost, for example, both place and voice in local, state, and national deliberations about the quality and character of public school education. By limiting their role to the support and advocacy of public schools, the denominations of the old Protestant mainline abdicated responsibility for constructively critiquing the mission and strategy of the nation's schools in the quest for the "best" education for all the nation's children and youth. Their constructive critique would have been useful, for example, when school leaders sought a new more inclusive moral center for their educational efforts. Instead, mainline Protestant churches generally supported uncritically the schools as they turned first, to principles and strategies of values clarification and then, to character education. When both failed to capture the public imagination, the old mainline Protestant denominations had nothing else to suggest.

Some academic religious educators did attempt to engage the churches in a conversation about their *religious* responsibilities in a comprehensively public education. Their efforts, however, failed to attract the attention of congregational and denominational leaders.[13] Although some leaders in these denominations attempted to challenge the increasing perception that the separation of church and state in public policy meant the exclusion of religion in the schools, they lacked the voice and place to be taken seriously. Nor were they in a position any longer to critique the increasing dominance of marketplace and consumer values in the distribution and selection of

---

13. Seymour et al., *The Church in the Education of the Public*; Hauerwas and Westerhoff, eds., *Schooling Christians*.

curriculum resources in either congregations or public schools. It did not take long for researchers to begin comparing the American high school to the "shopping mall," a comparison that could as easily have been applied to the youth ministries in many larger congregations.

Meanwhile, church agency staff and board members were not exploring the impact of the loss of the reinforcing structures of the public school on their own efforts to form the faith of the young people in their congregations. Rather than recognizing that the collapse of the Protestant strategy shifted full responsibility for education in forming the faith of their children back to the family and congregation, most of these denominations reorganized their educational structures in ways that only further fragmented, isolated, and frustrated those efforts in their congregations. We take up that story next.

The Loss of a Catechetical Culture of Formation in Congregations

The old mainline Protestant denominations generally ignored the collapse of the partnership of school and church. After 1960 most also began to curtail or dismantle their interdependent educational structures which had historically sustained and reinforced the faith formation of the children and youth in their congregations. Reasons for their actions varied, ranging from changing missional priorities, streamlining bureaucracies, cutting staff, downsizing budgets, negotiating theological conflicts, to the merging of denominations and the reorganization of their agencies. Changes from these actions not only altered the relationship of congregations to their regional and national education agencies; they often broke up the educational infrastructure that had long sustained local efforts. Their effectiveness as catechetical cultures of faith formation declined. A brief description of the impact of restructuring in one denomination—the United Methodist Church—may provide clues to the diminishing commitment to education as a theological practice in faith formation to be found during those same years in other denominations.[14]

14. Although many influences contributed to the decisions to dismantle existing educational structures in several of the larger old mainline Protestant denominations, denominational mergers provided unique opportunities for the reorganization of missional priorities and the realignment of institutional structures. Agencies in the congregation, regional judicatories, and national denominational offices responsible for education were in many instances realigned, downsized, or eliminated. The merging conference of the

The year 1968 was, in some ways, a good time for the merger of the Methodist and Evangelical United Brethren Churches. Radical social changes called for greater congruity between the historic mission of the churches of the land and the institutional structures embodying that mission. The continuing *relevance* of the church's mission was at stake. At the same time, it was the worst of times for creating new institutional structures. The intensity of the desire by many in the churches to disrupt historic patterns of racial and gender oppression and injustice, to subvert the authority and increase the managerial efficiency of the large bureaucratic agencies of the churches, and to accommodate the intensity of youth and student pressure for greater voice in church matters significantly overwhelmed those concerned with the *maintenance* of their most distinctive faith traditions and practices.

One of the most influential changes in the new denominational structure (along with the abolishment of racially segregated structures in the church and the racial integration of the denomination's judicatories) shifted the authority for initiating local ministries from denominational agencies to the congregation. The centerpiece of this legislation established a "council on ministries" in each congregation and corresponding structures in regional and national church bodies. The function of this council at each level of the church was to "*consider, initiate, develop, and coordinate proposals* for its strategy of mission."[15] For a Baptist the principle of local authority in this proposal would undoubtedly sound familiar. For the many Methodists who had heretofore relied on elected clergy and lay representatives and professional staff to establish national and regional priorities for

---

Methodist and Evangelical United Brethren Churches occurred in 1968. That merger had been preceded in 1957 by the merging of the Evangelical and Reformed Church and the Congregational Christian Churches into the United Church of Christ. In 1958 the Presbyterian Church in the USA and the United Presbyterian Church of North America merged. This new denomination then merged with the predominantly southern Presbyterian Church US in 1985. The Disciples of Christ also experienced a major change as some 3000 congregations withdrew between 1967 and 1969 over differences related to policies of baptism in the mission field. The Evangelical Lutheran Church in America was formed in 1988 through the merger of The American Lutheran Church, The Association of Evangelical Lutheran Churches, and The Lutheran Church in America. Robert L. Browning, Professor of Christian Education at the Methodist Theological School in Ohio from the 1960s into the 1980s details the story of the institutional changes in the education of the United Methodist Church in an unpublished and undated paper entitled, "Personal Reflections: About the History of Methodist Christian Education in the Twentieth Century" that was made available to this writer.

15. *The Book of Discipline of the United Methodist Church 1968*, parag. 153.

local ministries and programs, the change was dramatic. On the surface the relationship of congregation and denomination had been reversed. The responsibility for initiating and implementing local ministries now belonged to the congregation, but with a caveat. Priorities were to be consistent with denominational guidelines and resources were to reflect denominational standards.[16] The consequences of this shift have been many, including but not limited to the following:

- The new structure subsumed the Board of Education of the denomination into a new Board of Discipleship that brought into one agency oversight of education, evangelism, worship, stewardship, lay life, and ministry. While enhancing the potential for the coordination of programs, this decision radically curtailed national and judicatory education staff and diminished the general availability of educational expertise. It also signaled a preference for managerial rather than educational and theological competencies among professional and volunteer leaders.

- The new structure led to an emphasis on the marketing of curricular options rather than to a coherent vision for the formation of faith in congregations by locating with teachers and leaders the freedom and responsibility of choosing resources for teaching and learning. Knowledge of and identification with denominational traditions and practices declined.

- The new structure dismantled denominational networks of leadership training and gave that responsibility to congregations which for the most part, were not prepared to assume it.

- The new structure separated youth and college student ministries from the educational structures of the congregation and denomination contributing structurally to the precipitous decline and abandonment of denominational support for ministries with both age groups.

- The new structure separated the conversations about the purposes and practices of education in forming faith and equipping religious leaders in congregations from those same conversations in the denomination's colleges, universities, and seminaries.

16. Ibid., 91.

- The new structure did not plan for the impact of the disruption of these changes on the catechetical cultures of congregations in forming the faith of their children and youth.

Should it be a surprise, then, that when parents of children and youth did not find in many United Methodist congregations a coherent and effective educational ministry for their children, many left?

The impetus to these and related changes were many: a deepening lack of trust across the church over the exercise of external and hierarchical authority; a growing preference for individual and local initiative; an intensifying quest for recognition and power among those who had been marginalized and oppressed, and the increasing anger in many congregations over the involvement of denominational leaders in the civil rights movement and after 1968, in protests against the Vietnam War. The merger of two denominations also created an opportunity to address politically some deeply rooted tensions between national boards and agencies of the church (notably the Boards of Education and Evangelism), among church leaders in the South, North, and West; between historically black and white church traditions; and between those who identified themselves as theological liberals or conservatives.

Changes in the new denomination's educational agencies ironically subverted the cultural forces in congregations that supported and reinforced their educational efforts just as Ellis Nelson and other Christian education theorists were drawing attention to the influence of the life of the congregational in the formation of faith. "Christian faith . . . in the love of God," he had reminded us, "creates a divine compulsion in a person" to share self and possessions "with those who have not yet been liberated from the burden of sin or charged with the sense of divine purpose in their lives."[17] In communities of faith that compulsion is expressed through the confluence of preaching, worship, teaching, the care of others, and outreach to the larger community and world in the lives of those who participate in the congregation. It gives rise to a host of interdependent congregational activities from choir to camping programs, underscoring the congregation's desire to educate and thereby, hand on and incorporate a new generation into its faith and practices. It is the catalyst to a host of educational agencies, strategies, and resources linking congregations to their regional, national, and often some ecumenical partners in overlapping collaborative processes of forming faith lives and practice. The faith journey viewed from this

17. Nelson, *Where Faith Begins,* 15.

perspective becomes, as John Westerhoff observes, a "personal pilgrimage with companions in community."[18]

In her study of voluntary societies in the United States, Theda Skocpal points out these efforts in local settings have traditionally been strengthened and reinforced by regional and national networks of relationship and resources.[19] John Westerhoff calls the mutuality embedded in these inter-institutional processes "religious socialization." After the collapse of the partnership of public schools and the denominations of mainline Protestantism, however, these denominations generally dismantled or severely curtailed their regional and national networks.[20] Congregations soon discovered that without this wider network of resources and support, the educational challenge of nurturing among their members "a lifestyle which includes our total being as thinking, feeling, willing persons," was neither simple nor easy.[21] Restructuring, as done in the United Methodist Church, provided them with fewer and fewer opportunities to being "in pilgrimage with companions" across the denomination in that effort. They no longer knew whether or not their efforts contributed to any shared sense of what it might mean to raise up a new generation of Methodist followers of Jesus Christ.

When I visit congregations today, they often seem more involved in educating to *enrich the religious experience* of children and youth than to *nurture them as disciples of Jesus Christ.* More attention is given to what children *want* or *like* than to what children *need* to follow Jesus together through the challenges they daily face. Greater emphasis is placed on personal spirituality than on the renewal of some tradition of faith. More effort is given to creating what I once described as "a positive experience for students" that included everything "from having a good time in a hospitable place for young children to initiating a lively discussion among youth or adults."[22] When the subject matter of an educational event is religious these are appropriate goals. They enhance the quality of the educational experience. When these emphases dominate the values of the education in congregations, however, the outcomes are entertainment rather than transformation. They may facilitate the quest for spirituality permeating

---

18. Westerhoff, *Will Our Children Have Faith?*, 14.

19. For a larger discussion of her observation, see Theda Skopcal, *Diminished Democracy*, 153ff.

20 Westerhoff, *Will Our Children Have Faith?*, 14.

21. Westerhoff, *Living the Faith Community*, 92–93.

22. Foster, *Educating Congregations*, 28.

contemporary American culture—a quest Wade Clark Roof describes as the search "for something more than doctrine, creed, or institution."[23] But they do not enhance another quest directed to the *continuity* of the witness of their religious traditions to the grace of God's creative and redemptive activity in the world. The nurture of Christian discipleship from this perspective involves, as Craig Dykstra emphasizes, participation in the "means" of that grace.[24] That requires a lively and energizing culture of faith formation now missing in the education of all too many contemporary mainline Protestant congregations.[25]

With hindsight, I now contend, the dismantling of the infrastructure of congregational education involves a profound misreading of the dissolution of the partnership of the church and school forty years ago. The managerial and entrepreneurial model of congregational governance denominational leaders embraced assumed an abundance of resources in congregations, not only financial resources and useful spaces for learning, but a continuing pool of trained, faithful, and competent teachers and pastoral education leaders engaged in lively worship and vital mission. The architects of the new church organization, however, did not seem to realize that for the majority of congregations, the abundance of their resources did not exist in congregations but in the connectional support systems of the denomination. And just as these congregations received increasing authority for determining how they would educate their children, the denomination radically curtailed personnel and programmatic resources available to them.

Large and wealthy congregations were more effectively poised to accommodate these structural changes. They expanded their professional staffs to manage new and expanding responsibilities. Often following the advice of church consultants, however, they did not seek theological or educational expertise when hiring staff to guide their educational ministries. Instead they hired people known more for their effective administrative and managerial skills. In retrospect I am now aware that these decisions to create new structures for a new denomination had at least three pertinent and often contrary consequences.

1) The first loosened the connectional ties among congregations and between congregations and the denomination's educational agencies that

23 For a more extended discussion of this theme, see Roof, *A Generation of Seekers*; also his *Spiritual Marketplace*, 33–35.

24. Dykstra, *Growing in the Life of Faith*, 41.

25. This theme is addressed more fully in Foster, "Why Don't They Remember?," 89–112.

included among others, camps and conferences, publications, colleges, universities, and seminaries. Each congregation was now on its own as it attempted to figure out how to identify and draw on denominational and other resources to nurture the faith of children and youth.

2) The denominations lost the expertise of its professional church educators. In the new structure professionally trained and certified Christian educators were no longer advocates or agents of a denominational vision for its future through the education of its young people. Instead they became managers of locally based education programs. In some of the largest congregations they became directors of what many called program ministries. Managerial skills became more important than theological knowledge or pedagogical sensibilities. Nurturing personal religious experience became more important than building up communities of faith. Since the majority of smaller congregations lacked any professional leadership in Christian education, oversight of a congregation's educational ministry increasingly fell upon pastors who, in the new structure, had become not only the "pastor in charge," but also the manager of all the ministries of the congregation. Few pastors were prepared for this expanded and complex role.

3) The denomination and its congregations did not direct their attention to the challenge of determining how to maintain the most significant commitments, values, and practices of their religious heritage through the changes they had just instituted. Wade Clark Roof argues that "religious establishments" faced with change "have to make some shifts in strategies." Besides attending to the quest for the spiritual that characterizes contemporary religiosity, "they must find ways to institutionalize a greater level of deliberateness within their structures, a serious and on-going commitment to marshaling and monitoring their own resources" to maintain themselves over time. Roof, quoting Peter Berger, goes on to observe that this maintenance used to be the function of tradition, but in a secular and fragmented world, the task of "defining and perpetuating tradition becomes much more of a conscious undertaking and responsibility."[26] It requires a different way of looking at the resources for nurturing the faith of children and youth in any particular religious community—one that emphasizes channeling often limited but available resources toward that goal. The lack of attention to that task has contributed significantly to the collapse of a culture of faith formation in many of the congregations of the old Protestant mainline

26. Roof, *Spiritual Marketplace*, 311.

denominations. That, however, is not yet the full story of their complicity in the loss of their children and youth.

The Loss of a Compelling Narrative of God

It was not that the congregations of the old Protestant mainline denominations were not engaged with the topic of God during the upheaval of the 1960s and 1970s. Quite the contrary! God was the object of intense attention in much congregational education. Rather the problem, suggests J. B. Phillips in a popular book at the time, was that most people did not have a view of God "big enough for modern needs." It is impossible "for an adult," he adds, "to worship the conception of God that exists in the mind of a child of Sunday-school age, unless he is prepared to deny his own experience of life."[27] For Bishop John Robinson, whose widely-read *Honest to God* was published in 1963, the problem had more to do with the lack of attention to modern knowledge in the conceptions of God held by most people. With a different perspective James Cone argues in *A Black Theology of Liberation* in 1970 that the cultural and religious bias of white theologies prevented people in the churches from recognizing God's preference for the poor, oppressed, and marginalized. His point could be underscored by the popularity of Warner Sallman's painting of a blond and blue-eyed *Head of Christ* hanging in prominent places in a significant number of white and black churches.

The lack of attention among clergy and denominational leaders to the confusion created by the conflation of conflicting views of God in the worship practices of congregations underscores the critique of these and other writers at the time. In the congregation I was serving in the early 1960s, we regularly listened to scripture readings with images of God rooted in ancient cosmologies. We sang hymns with language ranging from Enlightenment emphases on the rationality of God to evangelical images of the intimacy of God to contemporary images of the justice of God associated with liberation theology and the civil rights movement. We recited prayers with language about God reflecting worldviews from at least the second, fourth, sixteenth, eighteenth, and occasionally the twentieth centuries. We listened to sermons often drawing on insights into the nature of God from the writings of contemporary Protestant and Catholic, black and white biblical and theological scholars.

27. Phillips, *Your God Is Too Small*, 2.

About this time, John Westerhoff, a prominent leader in Christian religious education, asked a question cutting through much of the debate for those of us concerned with the education of children and youth in the churches. Observing that we could no longer assume "the theological foundations that have undergirded our efforts are adequate for the future," Westerhoff asked, "Will our children have faith?"[28] That question had already haunted my early ministry. Every Tuesday afternoon ten to twelve senior high youth met in our home to explore claims about God embedded in the views of a number of contemporary writers. Our reading ranged from Tillich's relational view of God in *Courage to Be* to Albert Camus' depiction of heroic human response to tragic circumstances in the face of the absence of God in *The Plague*. Most, if not all these teens, were aware that Dietrich Bonhoeffer's vision of *Life Together* had significantly shaped the vision of that congregation's leaders about what it meant to be church together in Jesus Christ. Many could not have helped overhearing their parents discussing Bishop Robinson's critique in *Honest to God* of the persisting hold of ancient cosmologies on contemporary views of God.

In this congregation encounters with these different views of God tended to be seen as part of our quest as Christians toward a deeper and more comprehensive personal faith in God. Beyond this congregation and others like it, however, encounters of these various views often sparked intensely contested and sometimes vitriolic debates. Nowhere were those debates more intense than over the content of the curriculum resources produced by the denominations. Advocates of so-called conservative views of God robustly criticized so-called liberal images. Those espousing more liberal images rigorously challenged the adequacy and relevance of conservative images. African American, and later, feminist and womanist theologians roundly critiqued Eurocentric and male images of God. Some scientists and other secular writers observing the debate debunked the whole God discussion altogether. It was a difficult time to be a curriculum editor or regional or national Christian education staff member.

A typical example of their experience in the middle of the debate over these different views of God followed an editorial decision by the staff of *The Upper Room*, a devotional resource published by the United Methodist Church and distributed around the world. In the early 1980s the staff decided its visual images needed to be more inclusive. They needed to reflect more accurately the diverse racial and cultural heritages of its readers.

28. Westerhoff, *Will Our Children Have Faith?*

Photographs and art up to that point had depicted white people and reflected European American cultural values and experience. A decision to place on the back cover a picture of Jesus as a Native American Indian praying in the Garden of Gethsemane broke that tradition. The picture did not evoke much comment, perhaps because the ethnically specific features of the figure in the painting tended to be rather subtle.

Mary Lou Redding, editorial director of the *Upper Room*, recalls a quite different response to the May–June 1983 issue which included on the cover, artist Joe Cauchi's image of an explicitly Black Jesus in his painting *Jesus Blesses the Children*. She and her colleagues were deluged with letters and phone calls. Some were like the letter from an African-American man who appreciated this new image after years of seeing "pictures of a white Jesus all the time." Others were like the phone call from an angry and distraught European American woman who wanted to know "what in the world" had led *The Upper Room* to publish the picture. In her distress she repeated over and again, "I can't understand why you printed that picture." As the conversation continued, she began to cry. "My Jesus is not a Black man; my Jesus does not have thick lips." As she continued to cry she repeatedly emphasized she was not a racist. Cauchi's Black image of Jesus, however, was not an image of Jesus with whom she could identify. This was not a picture of the Jesus to whom she had committed her life.[29] The reaction of this woman was repeated many times as church editors increasingly challenged racial, cultural, and gender biases and stereotypes in the theological and educational assumptions of their denominational resources. Their editorial decisions to be more inclusive inevitably led both to praise and criticism, encouragement and frustration, anger and gratitude among their constituencies.

Two principles guiding curriculum development in several of the mainline Protestant denominations intensified the debate about God in the churches. A closer examination of the influence of these principles in the practices of the United Methodist Church may be illustrative. As we have already observed, the new structure of the denomination after 1968 located the authority for planning local ministries in the congregation and authority for the consistency of those ministries in standards and guidelines established by national church agencies. Curriculum resources produced by the denomination provided a theological and educational framework

29. Mary Lou Redding, email message to author, March 11, 2009.

for cultivating views of God faithful to the theological traditions of the denomination. That division of responsibility played into the growing distrust of local communities for policies and practices established by regional and national agencies. It pitted views of God central to national committee and staff discussions about the content of the denomination's curriculum resources against the views of many local church teachers and educational leaders. The result, as Jack Seymour wrote in 1982 at the height of the controversy, was "much confusion in the church over the meaning of curriculum." He locates the confusion in the "enlargement of the conception of curriculum in the minds of church educators, without a corresponding effect on the use of curriculum in the local church."[30] The consequence of that confusion, I suggest in another essay in that same monograph, was a "struggle for power" significantly rooted in competing views of God over what and how congregations were expected to teach.[31] It was already apparent that advocates for local authority on matters of what to teach and how were winning the struggle. Views of God congenial to denominational traditions continued to prevail in its published resources but many congregations increasingly chose resources leaders and teachers viewed as being easier to teach and more congenial theologically.

Another assumption about the function of curriculum embraced by United Methodist and other mainline denominations during the 1950s and 1960s increased the tension between national staff and congregational ways of thinking about God. Under the auspices of the National Council of Churches, sixteen denominations collaborated in what was called the Cooperative Curriculum Project. Together they produced a massive and systematic theological framework for developing age-appropriate resources for all age groups. Intentionally comprehensive and inclusive, it *integrated* diverse views of God, ministry, and the church into an overarching plan just at a point in time when overarching or dominant theories were being challenged as exclusive, patronizing, and patriarchal. Critics pointed out, for example, that this new plan for developing curriculum resources continued to privilege a particular view of God that was not shared by some Protestant Christians and excluded minority voices and perspectives.

The critique prevailed, and the goal of a comprehensive curriculum integrating concerns of the whole constituency of the church into its

---

30. Seymour, "The Untried Curriculum: The Story of Curriculum Development for Protestant America," 11.

31. Foster, "Curriculum and the Struggle for Power in the Church," 43ff.

resources for learning collapsed. Curriculum producers in the mainline denominations consequently responded to local demand with an increasingly market driven approach to curriculum distribution. With choices about resources now primarily located in congregations more attuned to local perspectives and practices, they were less likely to be bound together by a compelling view of God rooted in the theological traditions of their denomination. In this situation the quest for a compelling shared view of God in the denominations has been reduced, for the most part, to a competition for a share of the curriculum market.

Loss of Intergenerational Mentoring

During the past thirty years much attention has been given to a so-called generation gap by the staff of national and judicatory church agencies and many congregations. Conferences have been held, workshops sponsored, and resources produced to better understand and/or target groups variously designated as boomers, Gen-Xers, or millennials. An awareness of generational difference is not a new insight. I remember reading an article back in the 1970s contrasting the dominant messages shaping the consciousness of each of the generations after World War I in popular songs, advertising, political slogans, major social, economic, and political events, and new technologies. That article helped me understand why my depression-era parents *needed* to maintain a full freezer of food while I, who grew up in the 1940s and 1950s, was more concerned about the dangers of nuclear proliferation. As Wade Clark Roof concludes, differences in our pasts lead different generations to "see and act toward the world differently."[32]

Even as the literature delineating generational differences caught our imaginations, other writers had been equally intrigued by continuities across the generations. During the formative years of my ministry, I was reading Edgar Friedenberg's *The Vanishing Adolescent* and Paul Goodman's *Growing up Absurd*, and took note of their critique of cultural processes diminishing the meaning and significance of the years between childhood and adulthood. During these same years, church educators drew heavily on the work of Robert J. Havighurst, David Elkind, and Erik Erikson to describe the interdependence of the developmental stages in the life-cycle of a maturing person. Later we turned to James Fowler, who, building on the psychological insights of Erikson, Lawrence Kohlberg, and Jean Piaget and

32. Roof, *Generation of Seekers*, 3.

the theological insights of H. Richard Niebuhr, explored the structures and dynamics of faith across the life span. Successful negotiation of each of the developmental stages of faith required, he contended, a lively, responsive, and dependable intergenerational community.[33]

A number of interpreters of the adolescent experience in the United States during these same years observed, however, that these intergenerational ties were no longer functioning well for many young people. The effectiveness of parents, congregations, schools, and voluntary organizations in mentoring the identification of young people with their communities was declining. Educational theorist Henry Giroux, in a critique of the consumer captivity of adolescents, described young people as living in a "fugitive culture." More recently he concluded they were an "abandoned generation." Youth advocate Mike Males suggested a more sinister dilemma for contemporary youth in his descriptions of "The Scapegoat Generation." Journalist William Finnegan described forces in a "Cold New World" thwarting the futures of young people and crushing their spirits because they lack the intergenerational support systems needed for negotiating basic developmental tasks. A major study of high schools described a minority of students as "winners" and a majority of students as "losers" in the educational marketplace of the high school. Religious educator Michael Warren scathingly critiqued churches for their complicity in this appropriation of marketplace values in their own views of and approaches to young people.[34]

In her provocative study of congregations, *Welcoming Children*, Joyce Mercer describes the double messages congregations often communicate to young people. On the one hand, they are openly welcomed. Nowhere is this more evident than in the outpouring of goodwill during the baptism or dedication of a baby or young child. On the other hand, children all too often discover in churches that their welcome depends on not acting "like the children they in fact, are."[35]

Young people encounter another related set of double messages. They are told that through their baptism they participate in the church as "full members" and not as "members in training." That promise, officially embraced by denominations affiliated with the National Council of Churches

---

33. James W. Fowler's theory is most fully developed in *Stages of Faith*.

34. Giroux, *The Abandoned Generation: Democracy Beyond the Culture of Fear* and *Fugitive Cultures: Race, Violence, and Youth*; Males, *The Scapegoat Generation: America's War on Adolescents*; Finnegan, *Cold New World: Growing Up in a Harder Country*; Warren, *Seeing through the Media: A Religious View of Communications and Cultural Analysis*.

35. Mercer, *Welcoming Children*, 2.

in the adoption of *The Objective of Christian Education for Senior High Young People* in 1963, establishes (before we were conscious of the gender bias in our vocabularies) clear goals in the faith formation of youth.

> The objective for Christian education is that all persons be aware of God through his self-disclosure, especially his redeeming love as revealed in Jesus Christ, and . . . respond in faith and love—to the end that they may know who they are and what their human situation means, grow as sons of God rooted in the Christian community, live in the Spirit of God in every relationship, fulfill their common discipleship in the world, and abide in the Christian hope.[36]

In too many congregations, however, youth discovered that being a "full member" did not include either the education or the mentoring relationships needed for acquiring the knowledge and skills, habits and practices needed to live into the promises of this objective. The shared vision for the faith formation of young people in the National Council of Churches statement was not to be realized.

During the next forty years young people drifted away from the churches in ever greater numbers. Wade Clark Roof, Dean Hoge, Robert Putnam, and David Campbell, among other interpreters of boomer and Gen-X religious experience, tell the sociological and cultural part of the story. Putnam and Campbell, for example, take us back to the 1960s and remind us that it was a volatile moment in the nation's history. Young people were resisting all forms of authority, including that embedded in religious institutions. A "mélange" of contributing factors created the conditions for the growing tension between younger and older Americans. They included at least "the combination of unprecedented affluence and the rapid expansion of higher education, 'the Pill,' the abating of Cold War anxieties, Vatican II, the assassinations, the Vietnam War, Watergate, pot and LSD, the civil rights movement."[37] Putnam and Campbell and most of the other interpreters of the social movements of those years, however, do not draw attention to the complicity of the mainline Protestant denominations in the loss of their own children as they moved through adolescence into young adulthood.

Again let us examine more closely this story in the experience of the United Methodist Church. In 1968 the merging church approved a new vision for youth ministries. This vision was rooted theologically in the

---

36. *We Have This Ministry*, 12–13.

37. Putnam and Campbell, *American Grace*, 91, 94.

National Council of Churches statement *We Have This Ministry* and its *Objective of Christian Education for Senior High Youth.* In this action the church adopted the notion that youth are no longer to be viewed as the "future of the church," but are now to be considered full participants in the ministries of the church. It emphasized in the action as well a greater concern for the "relevance" of the church's ministries for youth while de-emphasizing any comparable concern for its continuity into the future through those same young people. They accomplished this shift by making the newly reconfigured United Methodist Youth organization an independent program agency of the denomination no longer related or accountable to the agencies responsible for guiding the church's educational mission. This new youth ministry structure shared the comparative autonomy of the United Methodist Women in the life of the church and had its own connectional network of relationships in regional and national church bodies.

This new structure departed radically from the prior authorization given to the Division of the Local Church of the Board of Education to establish and supervise youth ministries at all levels of the church. The structural underpinnings for a developmental curriculum across the life cycle, in other words, had been removed. The dismantling of institutional structures supporting an intergenerational notion of youth ministry continued with the reduction of church program resources for training leaders in youth ministry. Adults involved in youth ministries were no longer generally viewed as mentors. The network of professional leaders in youth ministry collapsed and jobs in youth ministry disappeared. Structural and financial support for campus ministries declined. The ties of congregations and judicatories with denominationally affiliated colleges and universities were loosened and, in many instances, abandoned.[38] The bonds linking ministries in the denomination's congregations to its colleges and theological schools fell apart.

Another set of decisions heightens the irony in the merging denomination's changing approaches to youth and college students. Several years after the merging conference of 1968, the denomination's General Board of

---

38. The full story of the reorganization of the program agencies of the mainline Protestant denominations during the 1960s and 1970s and its impact on their educational ministries has yet to be told. Some denominations loosened the bonds linking their educational agencies, and others, like the newly formed United Methodist Church, totally dismantled them. One thing is clear. The restructuring of the relationship of their educational agencies culminated in a diminishing commitment to education in the formation of the faith of their children and youth.

Discipleship instituted new studies on baptism and confirmation heightening consciousness across the church to the ritual function of intensifying the relationship of participants to the life of the congregation, its beliefs, traditions, and practices. The rite of confirmation, however, despite increasingly rigorous theological underpinnings, has tended to function in congregations more often as a rite of alienation from, rather than identification with, the life and mission of the church for many young people.

Three consequences have dominated my attention. In the first, the new structures for youth ministry effectively marginalized—and consequently, further alienated—vast numbers of youth whose "confidence in all institutions, including organized religion" had eroded significantly.[39] During the early 1970s junior and senior high youth attendance in congregational youth fellowships precipitously declined as did their participation in regional events. The denomination dropped national staff responsible for nurturing notions of Christian vocation among youth and cultivating future leaders in the ministry of the church. National conferences for high school and college students were no longer held. The church suffered a loss of advocates and mentors for youth in congregations, in regional judicatories, and in the national church agencies. Seminaries dropped their courses in youth ministry. As one deeply involved in youth ministry for many years, I often asked judicatory leaders to explain the declining numbers of participating youth. I invariably heard the response that it is not "quantity but quality we seek." That was an illusion. I saw three distinctive groups of teenagers who continued to participate in some congregation. They included those for whom church participation was a deeply held family value (sometimes over the protests of the teens), those who seemed to have an aptitude for things religious (often becoming leaders in new significantly reduced regional and national youth programs), and those who had not found a place in the increasingly competitive environment of consolidated public schools. The rest no longer participated in any regular fashion in the churches of their baptism. I also found in congregations and judicatories here and there across the country a few wise and committed mentors of youth struggling to retain something of the former ecology of youth serving organizations in the life of the church.

Increasing numbers of mainline denominational youth began to attend one of the para-church youth groups in their communities. This I found to be particularly interesting, because at the time, while these groups

39 Putnam and Campbell, *American Grace*, 94.

often understood the adolescent psyche better than many congregations, they also tended to be anti-adult, anti-denominational, and anti-intellectual. They existed, in one sense, to perpetuate adolescence and adolescent religiosity. Even a majority of their leaders were barely out of adolescence thereby often providing teenagers with helpful mentoring through the developmental crises of adolescence, but without the mentoring of wise elders needed for assuming adult roles and responsibilities. Although it should be noted, that over the years these same organizations sometimes allied themselves with denominational ministries, increased the role of adults in the lives of teenagers, and encouraged the engagement of adolescents in mission as well as in religious experience, they continue to diminish the role of religious tradition, critical theological reflection, and the interdependence of the generations. Is it any surprise then that young adults socialized into the value structures and practices of para-church youth organizations should—if they are interested—be attracted to congregations with worship and fellowship patterns like those they knew as adolescents?

The decisions to restructure the place of youth ministry in the church also shifted the role of adolescents in congregational life. Youth ministry as a program agency of the congregation became an option for youth participation—the opposite of the intention of denominational legislation. As an option for youth participation it increasingly relied on public relations and marketing strategies to recruit and retain the interest of young people. In this regard youth ministry became a choice for their involvement.[40] For great numbers of young people that choice was to leave the church that had already abandoned them.

Adaptive Challenges

The four losses I have been describing create the conditions for adaptive change in any congregation or denomination seeking a future through its children and youth. Margaret Mead some time ago describes those of us who live into the consequence of the constant changes of contemporary life—such as these—as "immigrants in time."[41] She was thinking about young people, but in this present age that is the experience of all of us.

40 Forces in the larger culture reinforced the notion that youth ministry could be an optional choice. The resulting commodification of the educational experience of teenagers has been described by Powell, et al., *The Shopping Mall High School*.

41. Mead, *Culture and Commitment*, 71.

None of us are "natives." None of us are fully at home in new situations or circumstances associated with some consciousness-transforming event. Mead had in mind the difference of consciousness among those born before and after the bombing of Hiroshima and Nagasaki. Those born before that event could not imagine the reality of war without survivors. Those born after the war could not imagine a war that did not include the possibility of the total annihilation of the earth's population. As one looks at the history of humankind, however, other examples of a similar gap in consciousness associated with other events come to mind: for example, between those born before and after Galileo's affirmation that the earth revolved around the sun, those born before and after the historical events we call the Reformation and Counter-Reformation, those born before and after Darwin's startling discovery of evolutionary patterns in all forms of life, those born before and after men walked on the moon, and those born before and after the development of Internet communication. A similar gap in consciousness exists among those of us born before and after the significant shifts of the past forty years in the traditions of faith associated with the old Protestant mainline denominations.

Differences between the views of those among us who are "natives" to some segment in time and those of us who are not creates a crisis for those concerned about education and the formation of faith. Mead makes the point. There are "no elders who know more than the young themselves about what they are experiencing."[42] This is a familiar insight to any grandparent seeking to catch up with the at-home-ness of their grandchildren in the world of computers, the internet, iPods, and Twitter or whatever new innovation will next dominate their attention. At the same time, those of us who are grandparents viewing the worlds of our grandchildren from our outsider vantage point may see limits and possibilities in their experience they cannot envision. Old and young, in other words, need the perspectives of each other. We both live in the possibilities and limits embedded in the differences of our time- and space-bound experience. This shift in our consciousness of our situation intensifies the adaptive challenges church leaders encounter in forming the faith of yet another younger generation. This is an explicitly pedagogical challenge focused on practices of ecclesially mentoring the formation of faith among the children and youth in our congregations. In the next chapter we begin to explore the content and shape of this challenge.

42. Ibid., 78.

Discussion Questions and Exercises for Personal and Group Discussion

1. What is meant in this chapter by "reinforcing structures"? What reinforcing structures exist to sustain and deepen the faith-forming education in the congregations with which you are most familiar?

2. How would you describe the intent of the term "catechetical culture" in your own words? What are the elements in the "catechetical culture" of a congregation with which you are familiar? And in the experience of a young person you know?

3. To what extent do the congregations you know continue to struggle with a shared compelling narrative about God in their quests to form the faith of their young people?

4. In the congregation(s) you know best, who are the adults mentoring the faith of young people? Where in the life of the congregation does that mentoring typically occur? Is their mentoring adequate to the challenges of cultivating the faith of the congregation's young people?

5. If possible, find a pastor or lay person who was deeply involved in the leadership of your denomination during the 1960s and 1970s. Explore with this person similarities and differences in their memories of changes made in the support structures for education in congregations with those described in this chapter. You might explore as well this person's perception of the legacy of those changes in the education of contemporary congregations.

6. If you would like to pursue the discussion of this chapter further, see if you can locate a copy of John H. Westerhoff's *Will Our Children Have Faith?* In what ways did he anticipate this chapter's critique of the church's education in forming the faith of children and youth?

Chapter Three

Learning in Faith Formation

Remember that you were a slave in Egypt and the Lord your God redeemed you from there.

Deut 24:18a

Introduction

With this chapter we take up the task of reclaiming a notion of learning conducive to forming faith in the education of congregations. The task will lead us to recover practice learning in a renewed emphasis on its interdependence with developmental and discovery learning in a congregation's education. I have suggested the Passover meal and its traditions as a model for envisioning the interdependence of learning in the faith formation of children in our congregations. The story of those traditions may be traced to the deuteronomic instructions of Moses to Israelites looking forward to establishing homes in the Promised Land. This story is filled with the promise of a lively future for Israel. It also served as a warning. Their longevity as a community depended on the extent to which it sustained and renewed those practices from generation to generation.

The warning is clear. If the elders of the community did not model faith for young people, if they did not guide young people through the conflicting values they would daily encounter, and if they did not answer the questions of young people that prompt stories of God's liberating activity, the community itself would wither and die. The continuing relevance of the covenantal faith of the Israelite people, in other words, depended on gathering their children into its practices of loving God with all their heart, soul, and might. In similar fashion, the continuing relevance of our faith traditions—Lutheran, Reformed, Anglican, Baptist, etc.—depends on the extent to which our congregations mentor the faith of our children and youth in the changing circumstances of the times in which we live. Although I did not recognize it at the time, I first began to consider the impact of the loss of attention to practice learning in a congregation's education while teaching a group of ninth graders in an old mainline Protestant congregation. That story highlights the task before us.

Why Don't They Remember?

During seminary I fulfilled my field education requirement in a large suburban New Jersey congregation. My responsibilities included teaching a Sunday school class and leading one of the youth groups. Approximately twenty-five ninth graders participated in the Sunday school class. Most had grown up in the congregation. Most came from families with a strong commitment to education and most already knew they were headed to college. Our study for the next six months was to be guided by a curriculum resource produced by the denomination on the life and teachings of the apostle Paul. I began the first session with a series of exercises to discover what they remembered about Paul and his writings from prior Sunday school classes, sermons, family discussions, and their own reading of scripture. Although they assumed I was asking them to identify someone in the New Testament, they could not answer a single question. "I don't know" and "I don't remember" were typical of the responses I received. I was mystified.

Most participated at least from time to time in the congregation's worship and had listened to readings from Paul's letters. They had heard sermons on texts from Paul's writings from an able preacher. Most had been in Sunday school classes as children taught by well-trained and gifted teachers using curriculum resources designed for use with specific age groups on the life and teachings of Paul. Most, if not all, had participated in membership training classes in the seventh grade in which they had again encountered some of Paul's writings and most had then taken on the responsibilities of church membership. The teaching they had experienced along the way in this congregation had valued their questions as catalysts to their learning. I assumed they would have remembered what they had been taught.

In the years following that incident, as a teacher in a number of different congregations, in denominational workshops, ecumenical conferences, and seminary classrooms I gradually realized that the not-remembering of students is a persistent challenge for teachers. I also became increasingly aware that teachers in all kinds of educational institutions spend much of their time and energy creating strategies to encourage student remembering: returning time and again to certain topics, subjects, or practices; exploring the same questions or issues from different vantage points and with different methods; repeating tasks over and again; creating ways to review and test student recall and comprehension.

And yet, the forgetting of these young people provides a clue to an important feature in the adaptive challenge facing any contemporary congregation seeking a future for itself through its children and youth. Beautiful spaces for teaching and learning, efficient organizational structures, theologically robust and age-appropriate curriculum resources, supportive parents, and creative strategies of teaching taking advantage of student curiosity had apparently not been enough to prepare this group of young people to recall basic information about the author of a good portion of the New Testament in the Bibles they had received in third grade and which they had used in Sunday school classes. Even more significant for a discussion of faith formation, their educational experience had not established for them a memorable relationship with Paul or his views on the life of faith with which they could identify. "Why didn't they remember what they had been taught?" That question prompted me to look more closely at the relationship of learning and remembering in forming faith.

To remember involves more than the recollection of information, narratives, conceptual frameworks, or skill sets. Its significance in the faith of Christians is highlighted in the celebration of the Last Supper of the disciples with Jesus. They are asked by Jesus—perhaps urged is a better word—to repeat the meal after he is gone "in remembrance of me." As Huston Smith observes, "The word 'remembrance' is laden with symbolism, for to re-member is to reassemble parts that have been sundered." Even as death would tear Jesus from the disciples, they would re-member or reassemble their experience with him in repetitive acts of "reenacting this Last Supper."[1] As the "body of Christ" a congregation participates in the

---

1. Smith, *The Soul of Christianity*, 68.

rhythmic patterns of symbolically re-assembling memories associated with that event. Those patterns re-echo in their experience as they gather and disperse, rehearse its stories, and participate in its rituals. Remembering, in other words, establishes both a goal for and is a key element in any faith-forming education. The cultivation of remembering in the faith of children and youth, however, has not been a primary concern of much of the education in the congregations of the old mainline Protestant denominations for several decades. This lack of concern may be traced, in part, to the lack of attention in these congregations to the way practice learning binds and sustains developmental and discovery learning in forming faith.

Inattention to Practice Learning

In the first chapter we explored the necessary interdependence of developmental, practice, and discovery learning in a faith-forming education. As the old mainline Protestant denominations abandoned education in forming the faith of their children and youth, however, they paid less and less attention to practice learning. I am convinced this again was not their intention. Although the memorization of Bible verses fell into disrepute during these years, I have no *memory* of any other discussions calling into question values associated with practice learning in workshops I led or conferences I attended. Rather the lack of attention to practice learning began in some congregations as an accommodation—or technical adaptation—to their rapid growth in the years following World War II.

Despite a much enlarged educational building, the congregation in which I was teaching this group of ninth graders, for example, could no longer gather its large and rapidly growing membership into a single worship service or Sunday school session. So, like many other congregations, it viewed its growth as a technical rather than an adaptive challenge. It instituted two worship services and two sessions of Sunday school to run concurrently. As the membership of the congregation continued to expand, folks now had a choice. Many families continued to participate in both worship and Sunday school, but the most popular choice by far, was for adults to attend worship while *sending* their children to Sunday school. This meant most adults in the congregation were not in formal learning groups and most children were not in worship. With two sessions of Sunday school the traditional intergenerational Sunday school assembly was abandoned as were most intergenerational pot-luck dinners, work projects, and mission activities. A specialist in Christian education on the staff freed the pastor for other responsibilities. Most congregational activities now occurred within specific age-related groups. The intergenerational relationships, the collective mentoring, and the repetitions of participating in practices of Christian fellowship alongside others were no longer part of the ongoing experience of most children or youth.

This congregation and its denominational leaders in Christian education, like many others at the time, primarily identified their efforts in faith formation with the administrative, curricular, and pedagogical practices of schooling. Expectations of the highly trained professional Christian education staff were similar to those of school principals and curriculum specialists. Expectations for the pedagogical expertise of volunteer teachers and leaders were similar to those of school teachers. Much time and energy were devoted to laboratory schools and workshops for training teachers and monthly planning meetings for adapting denominationally sponsored curriculum resources to the abilities and interests of the children and youth in their classes. Skillful supervisory support helped teachers and leaders through the relational, pedagogical, and theological challenges they faced.

Linking the processes of faith formation with schooling directed the attention of teachers and leaders to the cultivation of what Paul Connerton calls the "cognitive memories" of their students.[2] Teachers were urged to create age level communities of learning in which the *needs* and *questions* of their students were put in dialogue with the themes and goals of denominationally produced curriculum resources. Developmental and discovery learning strategies were emphasized. The focus of student learning centered on linking biblical narratives to the events and circumstances of their lives, using theological and ethical ideas and concepts in the quest for meaning, and recognizing virtues associated with the Christian life.

An emphasis on developmental and discovery learning, while crucial to the formation of faith, was not sufficient for the kind of remembering I was expecting from this group of ninth graders. Again Connerton suggests why this may be the case. To be meaningful or relevant the cognitive memories of our learning do not require "any information about the context" of the information or skill we are remembering. It does not assume an awareness of the situation, experience, or "episode of learning" some new body of information or set of skills in order for us "to retain and use" what we have

---

2. Connerton, *How Societies Remember*, 22.

learned.[3] Consequently it did not occur to me to ask these young people to recall when, where, or how they had previously encountered stories about the life of Paul or engaged his writing as catalysts to their remembering. I did not think it important to re-present something of the context of Paul's life or of his writings as catalyst or framework for their remembering. Nor did I consider the possibility of asking the youth to think about those times and places in the life of their congregation in which the influence of Paul might have been evident. A common example could have been a reading of the thirteenth chapter of First Corinthians in many wedding ceremonies. Instead, I assumed they could recall without reference to any historical or social context what they remembered about Paul and his contribution to the life and thought of the church and to the content of their own faith.

Missing from my assumptions as a teacher, and generally from the expectations of this congregation, was a conscious commitment to cultivating what Connerton has called the *habit memories* central, in this instance, to the thinking and practices of a life of faith.[4] We typically assume the memories embedded in our habits. They exist, for the most part, beneath the surface of our consciousness. They become evident whenever we do something, "more or less effectively" as "the need to do so arises."[5] For example, with little forethought or apparent effort we ride bicycles or drive cars through the busy streets of some city, connect the words on this page into coherent sentences and paragraphs, kneel or stand unselfconsciously at appointed times during worship, or pray spontaneously and deeply "from the heart."

Habit memories, in contrast to cognitive memories, are social and historical, embodied and contextual. They give shape and form to practices that distinguish the common life of families, congregations, and communities. They make up the patterns of greeting, singing, listening to the reading of scripture and sermon, and praying in worship. They influence the conduct of congregational meetings and ground expectations for the responses of church members to local, national, and international needs and crises. As we develop expertise in the exercise of these acts or practices of congregational life we are rarely aware of the continuing physical, emotional, or cognitive effort required to sustain the mental, spiritual, and physical habits embedded in them. We just do them. They seem to occur

3. Ibid.
4. Ibid., 22–23.
5. Ibid.

spontaneously, but in actuality they have been engrained in our minds and muscles through often disciplined repetition. They seem simple, but in reality, their complexity is absorbed into levels of expertise encouraged and reinforced by the deliberate coaching of mentors and the informal affirmation of others. They feel natural, but in truth, they have been tested and refined over time as we have engaged them in different situations and under varied circumstances.

As I pondered the function of habit memory in the practices of faith my thoughts wandered one morning to my efforts to maintain an aerobic discipline of swimming. I came to swimming late—in fact, after I turned forty. As a skinny child swimming lessons in an unheated pool on a hill swept by cool winds in my hometown had been lost on me. I spent far too much time shivering in my towel. I did learn enough to get around in the water but little more. After turning forty, however, my doctor urged me to take up swimming. So I began heading to a local pool three times a week. It was hard work. I was not comfortable in the water. I was self-conscious about holding up other swimmers in my lane. Every stroke took effort. My arms and legs felt like weights. Yet with *practice* over the next several months and years I eventually worked my way up to the point where I could swim a mile.

After we moved to another city I did not locate another pool so my swimming was limited to the pools of motels when we traveled. On those occasions I discovered both my skill and my confidence had significantly decreased. Then we moved again and I had access to another pool. It took at least six months before I could once again swim a mile. Then we moved once again and my work responsibilities did not leave space in my daily schedule for swimming. So when I finally did have an opportunity to return to a pool I had to learn all over again how to be comfortable in the water. It took several months before I once again became proficient enough to swim even half a mile. In the middle of this last effort, someone who learned to swim as a child, was on swimming teams through college and now swam five miles two or three times a week as an adult, watched my swimming effort. Like a good coach he suggested a simple change in my stroke. Suddenly the effort was much less. My stroke was more powerful. And I felt even more confident with the level of my expertise in the water.

I am convinced that learning to swim and learning to pray, or be compassionate, hospitable, generous, or any of the other practices Dorothy Bass has highlighted in *Practicing Faith,* have many similarities.[6] We learn them

6. Bass, ed., *Practicing Our Faith.*

best as we are developmentally ready to engage them as children, youth, or adults: hence, the important link between developmental and practice learning. So our granddaughters, each of whom began swimming as young children, are already much more comfortable and proficient in the water than I will ever be. We learn the complex patterns of action and thought in any practice most effectively over a significant length of time, preferably with the support of mentors and the encouragement of peers. If we should cease or skip practicing the habits of the practice they become stiff and flabby. We become overly conscious of the effort involved. We may even lose the ability to engage in the practice—as my father, once a powerful swimmer in his youth—discovered after the age of eighty-five when the habits of the practice were no longer embedded in the muscles of his body. He could describe the actions of swimming, but he could not perform them. His body had *forgotten how* to swim. In similar fashion when we no longer continue to practice praying, singing, serving others, being hospitable or generous the quality and effectiveness of our practice diminishes. If we are not careful, we forget—not just cognitively, but in our bones and muscles; indeed, in the very depths of our being. When that happens we no longer re-assemble the parts that make up the practices that had at one time given form and meaning to our faith.

Habit memories have one more function pertinent to this discussion. They link or bind us into families, neighborhoods, congregations, work groups, and volunteer groups that make up our communities of remembering. We participate in a practice as we imitate the habits of others. We refine them as we assess the extent to which they are valued or appreciated by people who are important to us. We celebrate them in the excellence of our performance with others. We are guided to ever greater competency in the practice by mentors and coaches and the affirmation of those around us. Some mentoring occurs informally. This is evident in the experience of the young child who constantly looks back to a parent or older sibling for signs of approval and affirmation in the midst of some new effort.

Other forms of mentoring are more formal. Coaches of athletic teams, dance troops, or speech teams, conductors of choirs and other forms of musical ensembles, and leaders of prayer retreats bring expectations of the performance they seek in the guidance they give to the learners in their care. Similar expectations may be found in the liturgical leadership of a pastor, the conduct of a meeting by a committee chair, and the modeling of expectations by a teacher in a classroom. Although we develop the habits of our practices in a variety of ways, we become aware of our proficiency, as Connerton observes, in "the fact of the performance" of our practice. It is then we "recognise and demonstrate to others" we "do in fact remember" the knowledge and skills of the practice.[7]

In the practice of our habits of faith our minds are "predisposed with a framework of outlines, of typical shapes of experienced objects" inherited from the past and embodied in the knowing and doing of the community or congregation in which we participate.[8] These shared predispositions to our knowing and doing become catalysts to resources for new knowledge and new skills, hence the crucial link with discovery learning. They guide our thinking and influence our actions, shape the perceptions we have of ourselves within the congregation that is the context of our teaching and learning, provide data for testing what we know and do not know, and clarify the depth and extent of our commitment to the content of those predispositions. They give impetus and form to how we think about ourselves in relation to those who both share and do not share those expectations. We are conscious of some expectations and not of others. Some are perpetuated through ritual. Others hover beneath our consciousness in the stories we tell, in the values that influence our decisions, and in the skills that carry us through the shared practices that make up the collective life of the groups or communities with which we identify.

In a faith-forming education these expectations give distinctive form to the patterns of continuity and transformation of congregational faith from one generation to the next. They originated in the experience of people recorded in the Bible and the early centuries of the church. More recently they have been distinctively influenced by a congregation's denominational heritage. With each passing generation they are handed on and renewed. As we encounter these expectations in our congregations they connect our faith journeys both with those who came before us and those who will follow us. These mediated expectations have an *ecclesial* shape highlighting our identities as recognizably Catholic, Orthodox, Wesleyan, Reformed, Lutheran, or Baptist or as a member of some new configuration of traditional and contemporary religiously social practices. The ecclesial shape of these practices, in other words, is both context and catalyst to a congregation's faith-forming education.

---

7. Connerton, *How Societies Remember,* 22.

8. Ibid., 6.

Challenges to Habit Practice Learning

As I reflect back on the church education experience of the ninth graders in my seminary field education placement, I am now aware they had had few opportunities to develop habits of faith practice conducive to the appropriation of the congregation's teaching about Paul with which they could identify. Despite an exemplary Sunday school, little else in the context underscored and reinforced the importance of their encounters with Paul and his writings for their own faith. Most families in this congregation had moved to this community. They had left the intergenerational ties of extended families in the Midwest, South, and Northeast to work in the corporate world of the metropolitan area. The congregation did not cultivate intergenerational mentoring relationships outside its formal educational structures. These ninth graders knew few adults in the congregation other than their parents, the director of the children's and youth choirs, the Boy Scout troop leader, and the Sunday school teachers and youth leaders whom they would see for a year or two.

The age-segmented isolation of the congregation's teaching and learning was further compounded by the structure of the curriculum resources used in the Sunday school. In an effort to be responsive to the dynamics of developmental and discovery learning, they had been designed by denominational leaders to repeat themes in age-appropriate ways. So these young people had previously encountered curriculum units on Paul in the third and sixth grades. This meant the congregation's teaching for children divided their learning into discrete, sequential, and self-contained units. Little in the life or formal education of this congregation, in other words, cultivated habits to hold and carry memories from one educational moment into the next.

Neither were there many places outside the Sunday school and youth group in this congregation where these young people were systematically mentored or coached into practices of faith associated with the heritage of this congregation. Although most families in the congregation strongly supported its efforts in teaching their children and many parents took a turn teaching in the Sunday school, few families assumed responsibility for any sustained formal religious instruction in the home. Few parents engaged in any formal religious education for themselves. Although prayer at certain public school events and religious music for holiday concerts were still common, values of competition, privilege, and individualism dominated the agenda for students in the local schools, undermining congregational efforts to inculcate among them values of compassion, collaboration, and reconciliation embedded in their faith tradition. The congregation, moreover, had not yet recognized the shifts taking place in the social location of old mainline Protestantism in the life of the nation. It had not yet realized that if it wanted its children to remember its deepest values, commitments, and practices, no other agency in the community could be relied on to assist them in this effort.

Challenges facing this and other congregations in the 1960s are more complex for congregations in the twenty-first century. New technologies have transformed when, where, and how we meet and communicate with each other. We are more likely to encounter something of the range of the cultural, religious, and ideological diversity of the nation in the communities where we live and where our congregations gather. We are confronted by alternative value systems and practices associated with other great religious traditions of the world and the dominant economic and social structures of the community. In this situation the cultural influence of mainline denominations has declined to the point that each exists as only one of many options for a life of faithful belief and practice.

Another challenge in its present form is comparatively new and requires a more expansive discussion. In recent years new technologies have transformed the world of children and youth through what philosopher of science Albert Borgmann has called "a virtual fog of cell phones, pagers, beepers, personal CD players, digital cameras, and video displays."[9] Most middle school children in North America now have cell phones. Many have Blackberries and iPhones. Most regularly *text* their friends and often their parents as well! They do much of their school work on a computer and use the Internet to conduct most of the research for their classes.

The influence of new technologies in shaping the mind and character of a generation of young people in new directions is not a new phenomenon. The printing press transformed the oral practices of medieval faith formation with practices centered on the ability to read. By the time the Puritans were sailing toward their vision of a *New* England, their children were not only being introduced to their traditions of faith through long-standing daily oral practices of prayer, Bible reading, moral prescription, exhortation, and expository preaching, but new publishing techniques meant primers were increasingly introducing them to the alphabet with

9. Borgmann, "On the Blessings of Calamity and the Burdens of Good Fortune," 7.

moral and religious sayings. Story books would soon be available to high-light the virtues of the faithful life and reinforce catechetical instruction. Reading was becoming as important as oral instruction in any education concerned with the formation of faith. Perhaps most significant, with books the learning of young people was no longer limited to the knowledge and skills of their pastors, parents, and other adults in their congregations or communities.

Subsequent technological innovations from the steam engine, train, and automobile to the airplane and space shuttle and from the telegraph to the telephone, radio, film, television, computer, and Internet have also increased the physical and relational distance between the elders of a community and its young people. A thought experiment I often used in my teaching may illustrate the challenges from technological innovation in congregations seeking to pass along their values, commitments, and practices to their children. In this experiment I asked students to contrast how modes of travel at different points of our history affected what they would know about the countryside through which they traveled. In the exercise I asked them to contrast what they might see and experience as they walked the ninety miles between two cities, drove the distance in an automobile, and flew over it. It did not take long to build lists that ranged from being able to recognize birds and name the varieties of trees while walking to tracing the path of rivers across the landscape while flying. It also did not take long to make the observation that each mode of transportation involved significantly different perspectives, emphasized different kinds of knowledge, and made use of different skills.

One could expand the exercise to consider differences of influence on the ways we perceive and make sense of the world around us when we communicate with a friend by letter, telegraph, telephone, or text message, or organize our interactions with each other by a view of time embedded in the sun dial, analog or digital clock. Borgmann has argued that "for most of us the progress" associated with technologies like these "has been a transition from the engagement with things in their contexts to the consumption of commodities that are available anywhere and anytime."[10]

This transition may be most visible in the impact of the technological shift from the mechanical to the digital time piece on how we think about ourselves in the contexts in which we find ourselves. Before the invention of digital watches, when asked for the time, we would say that it is "almost

10. Ibid., 22.

nine-thirty" or "half-past nine." We tended to view a given moment in relation to some larger sweep of time. With our digital watches, and for most young people, their digitized cell phones, we now say it is "9:28." The focus of our attention is on the specific moment displayed on our watch. Its temporal context is no longer relevant. The technology of the digital watch, in other words, has not only changed the way we identify the relationship of any moment in time to the past or future, but also in ways we more generally understand our relationship to the passage of time. It highlights, above all else, that we live in the present moment.

A similar change is also taking place in the ways we relate to the information that informs our discussion or thinking about almost any topic. If we want to know the meaning of a word, for example, we no longer look it up in a book called the dictionary which locates a word in relation to all other words with similar spellings. Rather we type the word into our computers and a definition appears on the screen. Typically it is surrounded by product advertising and not by related words of similar spelling or meaning. In similar ways we can instantly *access* information simply by typing into our computers a few key words instead of setting up *research* guidelines to find out what we want to know. The information we receive often tells us nothing about its author, the context or motivation of the author in producing that information, or the methodology by which the author obtained the information. It stands alone and on its own. The computer and the internet have transformed, in other words, our relationship to the information that fills our conversations, the agendas of our meetings, and the curriculum of our schools.

New technologies have also changed our relationship to the options available to us in our work and leisure. The automobile, as one example, made it possible for us to commute to work, consolidate schools, expand curricular options and school activities, and develop very large congregations. It increased our options for leisure time and for church affiliation. The computer and various telecommunications technologies only expand even more the range of our options. The impact on our consciousness or the ways we relate to information, other people, places, events, and even God is significant. The options now before us become commodities, in Borgmann's terms. They await our choice. Whether words, ideas, material objects, or relationships, they can be consumed and then discarded when we are no longer interested or need them. As we work our way through the options before us, the proficiency of our skill in using the technology is emphasized over our knowledge of the relationship of what we are doing to its context and our commitments to the choices we have made.

We can see the significance of this observation in the young person who knows almost intuitively how to program the television or solve a technical computer problem but is unable to make connections between the life and teachings of Paul and the lived experience of the church in the past or the present. To put the challenge even more forcefully, in this technological environment, the function of contextually focused remembering no longer seems important to many young people. Why should they feel the need to remember anything about Paul and his teachings when all they have to do to know something is to "Google it"?[11]

Why? The answer to that question lies at the heart of this book: the life of faith in the God who creates and redeems is a relational faith, a historical faith, a faith embedded in the lively contexts of communities of faith over time. It has a past and, if appropriated in ways to renew the life and ministry of those communities, it will have a future. The point, as Borgmann notes in his critique of the limits of technology, is that "Each of us is a unique and inexhaustible locus of convergence and transmission through our ancestry, both evolutionary and historical, through our descendants, through the sensibility of each of our organs, through our pleasures and pains, through our wounds and our scars, through our attacks and our embraces."[12] So in the midst of the technologies that do so much to enhance the richness and variety of our contemporary lives, Borgmann adds, we turn, for example, to the artificial intelligence of "an intelligent computer the way we now turn to the Psalms or to *Chicken Soup for the Soul*." But it is not to the intelligence of the computer that we actually do turn. It is to "the writers' experiences of pain and their fortitude in the face of it" made accessible to us through the computer that we seek and which truly "gives us a sense of trust and solace."[13]

It is more. In the way the writers of these two texts embrace and draw on the traditions of dealing with pain in all of its personal, relational, and historical manifestations we find in their images, symbols, and words, the power to comfort, heal, and transform our lives. But it is still more. The

---

11. Katherine Turpin argues this ability is a major feature of the faith of the consumer culture that dominates the imaginations, indeed, the religious imaginations, of young people; for an extended discussion, see *Branded*.

12. Borgmann, "On the Blessings of Calamity and the Burdens of Good Fortune," 13.

13. Ibid., 13–14.

memories associated with these texts and others like them embedded in the practices of a congregation or religious tradition function in some transformative way in our lives. We experience them as hope or meaning. These memories cannot simply be accessed, they must be embodied. This brings our discussion back to the role of practice learning in cultivating the remembering embedded in our practices of faith.

Habit Practice Learning

I have been contending that congregations seeking a future for themselves through their children and youth must reclaim in their education, developmentally appropriate practice learning habits of faith. I came to this insight and conviction through another experience of teaching. This time I was with a group of children in another congregation in another city in another part of the country more than thirty years later. It happened this way. In the mid-1990s I, along with several students from the Candler School of Theology in Atlanta, had completed a study of three congregations intentionally embracing racial and cultural diversity as an integral aspect of their identities and mission.[14] After we completed our research and written up the report of our findings, my wife and I, with a deep appreciation for the vitality of their worship and mission, decided to join the one closest to our home. In this congregation, leaders were seeking someone to take on the task of teaching the children in its Sunday school. It had been several years since I had been directly involved in an educational ministry with children. It seemed this might be an opportune time to discover its new challenges and possibilities. So I volunteered as did an educator who was also a grandmother and refugee from wars in Liberia. Over the course of several years two or three mothers who had also fled the wars in Liberia and a seminary student from Mississippi joined us for a time. The challenge before us was a big one.

The class included some twenty children ranging in age from six to twelve, with a corresponding range in reading and writing skills. Differences in our cultural and racial backgrounds as teachers were compounded by the diversity of culture and experience among the students. They came from families either from or with roots in Africa, Asia, the Caribbean, and North America. Some of their families were political or economic

14. The report of this study may be found in Charles R. Foster and Theodore Brelsford, *We Are the Church Together*.

refugees from embattled and impoverished nations. Some families in the congregation had both Christian and Muslim members. Questions about the immigrant status of the refugee families, challenges to their economic viability, and adjustments to a strange and new society intensified the sense of instability and fragility many of these children experienced. Their parents generally found in the congregation a welcoming place. That was less true for their children.

In other words, we faced several deep pedagogical and theological challenges:

- Providing a hospitable place in which a group of children with widely disparate backgrounds and experience might feel welcome and at home.

- Accounting for the cognitive, spiritual, physical, and emotional developmental differences of some twenty children ranging in age from six to twelve.

- Accounting for the racial, cultural, and language differences of the children and in ourselves as a teaching team as well as differences associated with the contrasting experience of the children and ourselves with the use of the computer and other new technologies.

- Accounting for the range of the knowledge of and experience with Christian tradition among the children, which did not necessarily correspond to their developmental ages.

- Accounting for differences in American and immigrant family assumptions about the place and role of children in the congregation and the role of adults in the care and supervision of children.

- Envisioning pedagogical practices through which these children might develop the language and skills to participate with increasing confidence in the life and mission of the congregation.

- Helping these children develop the kind of faith knowledge use, through which they might remember what they had been taught and the ability to practice a growing and deepening faith in God in and beyond the congregation.

We met with the pastor, the worship and education committees to explore these challenges. Several of our decisions are pertinent to this discussion. Since the pastor used the lectionary in his liturgy and sermon preparation, we chose a lectionary-based curriculum resource produced by one of the old mainline Protestant denominational publishing houses to link what we were doing in the Sunday school class with the experience children had in worship. This made sense for many reasons. Among them, it kept our educational efforts focused on cultivating the relationship or faith of these children in God. It linked the nurture of the faith of children with worship as the central and unifying practice of the faith of the congregation. It provided a sustained and systematic course of learning through the cycle of the lectionary and its use in the congregation. It focused our attention on creating a learning environment emphasizing the mutuality of developmental, discovery, and practice learning in an education directed to the formation of faith. It was also a practical decision. Most parents, both American and foreign born, assumed their children should be in worship from an early age, but they did little constructively to alleviate their restlessness in worship.

With a commitment to helping the children remember what we were attempting to teach, we then chose to limit our attention to the lectionary readings for one Sunday of the month for the entire month. We drew on suggestions from the curriculum resource to create a series of exercises through which the children might encounter the same texts, the same themes, and the same practices several times each Sunday during that month. We attempted to be responsive to the developmental learning patterns we discovered among the children by accounting for the range of age, experience, and ability of the children in the learning exercises we created. This meant we typically had two or three different activities going on at the same time. We encouraged older children to assist younger children. We encouraged children to draw on their racial and cultural heritages to express and give form to their learning and to enrich the experience of all of us. We made space for children to articulate their questions and then posted them on a large sheet of paper on the wall so we would not forget them as we planned future sessions.

Since the worship committee selected a "hymn of the month" to be sung each Sunday for a whole month, we practiced the hymn in our Sunday school class, often memorizing one of its verses in the process. In each session the children also worked at memorizing a portion of one of the biblical texts for the month as well as prayers and the creed used each Sunday in worship. Since we drew on many strategies for memorizing, the children typically experienced our efforts as more of a game. We also gave copies of the material being memorized to parents so they could, if they chose to do so, reinforce our efforts at home. And we would return time and again to previously memorized work in an effort to sustain the memory over the course of the year.

On the Sundays when the texts we had been exploring shaped the liturgy for the morning, the children posted any work related to the lectionary texts they had done in one of the hallways of the church for everyone to see. Since the hallway was the shortest route from the sanctuary of the church to one of the parking lots, many adults viewed their maps and artwork and read their stories. During the congregation's worship on the designated Sunday for the lectionary readings they had been studying, they either recited or dramatized one of the scripture lessons or sang one of the verses from the hymn they had been learning. Since the more advanced readers in the class had learned how to look up the texts they were studying, they began to look up and follow on their own initiative the reading of the lessons in their Bibles during worship.

I will never claim the challenge we took on was an easy one or that class sessions were systematic and orderly. And yet, after several months we noted several things happening. Adults in the congregation who had no other connection to the children began seeking them out to talk to them, to affirm something they had done in the leadership of worship, or to comment on something they had created and posted on the hallway wall. They began to address children by their names. Most children no longer expressed resistance to participating in the worship services of the congregation. Since elements of the liturgy were now increasingly familiar to them they were actively participating in the parts they knew. They began to urge the pastor to repeat in worship hymns they now knew. Undoubtedly because he invited comment, some children began to share with him something they had heard in his sermons. Patricia Benner describes this increasing proficiency in the congregation's practices of worship as "knowledge use" as contrasted with "knowledge about."[15] What was learned in class could be *used* in the congregation's worship. It had become contextually relevant. It intensified the bonds of children and adults in a shared set of liturgical practices. We had engaged the children in a nascent stage of embodied knowing. They were participating in the faith practices of the congregation.

We did not notice for some time what may have been the most interesting change in the attitudes of the children. One morning we realized that for several weeks we had not heard any of the children complaining about how "boring" worship was. As we pondered what this might mean,

15. Benner, *Educating Nurses*, 83.

we gradually came to the conclusion that for these children at least, declarations of boredom indicated lack of familiarity and therefore, a lack of confidence, in using the knowledge or skill required in a given situation. It underscored their lack of identification with whatever is "boring." I later discovered this to be true of my grandchildren as well. A game was "boring" when they did not understand the rules or lacked the skills to compete proficiently. A book was "boring" when they lacked knowledge of the background or context to make sense of the story or the language skills to follow the storyline. Worship was "boring" when they lacked familiarity with what the congregation was doing; when their lack of familiarity and competence alienated them from its forms, its words, its actions.

In this teaching experience with a group of children we may note several features of practice learning in a faith-forming education. Social scientist Etienne Wenger notes the concept of practice "connotes doing." Developing the habits of a practice, consequently, occurs in the repetitive doing of some part of the practice. But it is not just the doing in and of itself. It is doing with a consciousness of its "historical and social context." In this instance that context is a congregation within a specific religious tradition "that gives structure and meaning" to its doing the practice.[16]

At this point Robert MacAfee Brown's view of faith once again becomes helpful. Christian faith "stands in a special relationship" to something that happened in the past. That something symbolized for Christians most powerfully in the life, death, and resurrection of Jesus Christ gives impetus and urgency to God's persistent quest to be in covenantal relationship with humanity. This means, as Bass and Dykstra observe, "our daily lives are all tangled up with the things God is doing in the world."[17] This suggests the challenge for us is "to figure out how to pattern our practices after God's" in the hope we might "become partners in God's reconciling love."[18] This is not something we arbitrarily choose to do. It is something we do as we participate in the contemporary struggle of a religious tradition to creatively appropriate, as Brown has again suggested, its perspectives, values, and practices in the midst of the expected and unexpected events of our lives. That suggests we do not engage in the effort to pattern our practices on what God is doing in the world on a whim. Nor is it something we do now and then, here and there. If it is to nurture a future for the

16. Wenger, *Communities of Practice*, 47.

17. Dykstra and Bass, "Times of Yearning, Practices of Faith," 8.

18. Ibid.

congregations of a religious tradition, it must be *practiced* or rehearsed in each generation, time and again, over and over, year after year.

The practices of worship, as one example of how we might pattern our practices on those of God, originate in the fundamental human need for relationships that give meaning and purpose to the challenge of living with hope and trust through whatever conditions influence our daily experience.[19] The rehearsal of some of those patterns established a structure of predisposed expectations for engaging the children of this congregation in practicing habits embedded in its practices of worship. The patterns in those practices have their roots in the renewal of those practices among worshiping Christians and Jews through many centuries. Our intent as teachers and as a congregation involved more than the blind repetition of those inherited actions in this congregation's worship and definitely something other than the creation of something new and different that might entertain in the quest to sustain the interest of the children. Rather it was to empower the children of that congregation to participate competently and creatively in its worship in ways appropriate to their developing capacities for worship and responsive to the questions they were asking along the way.

The dynamics of the pluralism of our communities and the transformative power of new technologies intensify the challenge for congregations seeking to pattern their practices on the practices of God. No longer can congregations assume those patterns are generally present in the cultural experience of young people and their primary task is to assist in the socializing influences of that culture. Rather, if their children are to come to the point where they can envision themselves as bearers of the congregation's faith heritage and agents of its faith in the future, then the congregation must be much more self-conscious about how it engages its young people in the patterns of God's practices than it has in the past. This shifts the emphasis from learning to *know about* to what Patricia Benner has calls the *situated learning* that occurs when the present of our doing is taken seriously in its historical and social context.[20]

This requires that any congregation seeking to cultivate the situated knowing of a faith-forming education must examine the extent to which

19. Ibid., 6–7.

20. Benner, *Educating Nurses*, 41–42. Benner's notion of situated learning reflects Wenger's understanding of the primacy of the dynamics of "everyday existence, improvisation, coordination, and interactional choreography" in the "construction of individual or interpersonal events" ranging from conversation to activities; cf. Wenger, *Communities of Practice*, 13.

its life and mission are conducive to the kind of faith knowing and doing it seeks in its young people. Furthermore it must assess the extent to which its educational structures and strategies are mutually responsive to the developmental capacities and possibilities children and youth bring to their learning, the heritage that gives rise to and shapes the faith practices of the congregational community, and the creative and redemptive activity of God calling its members to live into the mystery of its possibilities.

This observation draws our attention even more closely to the content of the contexts of education in which the interdependence of developmental, practice, and discovery learning is emphasized in the formation of faith. Describing that content is my task in the next chapter. The focus of my attention will be on a set of practices that constitute the catechetical culture of a congregation directed to the formation and transformation of faith.

Discussion Questions and Exercises for Personal and Group Reflection

1. In what ways might "remembering" be considered a theological practice? Compare the kind of remembering encouraged in Deuteronomy 6 and in Jesus' instructions to the disciples during the Last Supper with the most common practices that cultivate the practice of remembering in the congregation you know best.

2. Describe a moment in which you experienced or observed an educational event that effectively cultivated the interdependence of developmental, discovery, and practice learning.

3. Identify a habit memory central to the practice of your own faith. Trace the people, events, and influences that helped you develop this habit. What implications do you see in your own experience for congregations seeking to cultivate the faith of their children and youth?

4. New communication and educational technologies provide new opportunities and threaten traditional ways of educating for faith. Choose a relatively new technological innovation. Identify ways it confronts congregations with technical and adaptive challenges in forming habit memories in the practice of faith.

5. If you would like to explore the themes of the chapter in greater depth, select a curriculum unit designed for children or youth in some church

setting. Review it carefully in order to identify the attention it gives to the interdependence of developmental, practice, and discovery learning in forming the habit memories of children and youth. How would you describe its strengths and limitations as a resource for a congregation's education in forming faith, based on your findings?

Chapter Four

Congregations as Catechetical Cultures

Keep these words that I am commanding you today in your heart. Recite
them to your children and talk about them when you are at home and
when you are away, when you lie down and when you rise.

Deut 6:6–7

Forming Faith in Catechetical Cultures

In the previous chapter I asked "why don't children and youth in our
churches remember more of what they have been taught?" Typically
questions like this one have been addressed in the educational literature as
the problem of the teacher, the curriculum, or the school. Sometimes it is
attributed to parents. The challenge for congregations, I contended, actually has more to do with their loss of attention to the dynamics of learning
in faith formation—particularly to the interdependence of practice with
developmental and discovery learning. In the pages that follow, I will argue
that the difficulty young people have in remembering has an even deeper
source. It can be stated as follows: if the context of faith formation does
not reinforce or sustain the learning it seeks to cultivate, the chances of the
remembering at stake in forming our collective identities as followers of
Jesus Christ diminishes significantly. Children and youth remember what

is important to them. Just as significantly, they remember what is important to the communities with which they most identify.

This insight unfortunately has been lost in the current debates over education generally, and especially in discussions about forming and transforming the faith of the children and youth in our churches. Teachers, classrooms, and prepared curriculum resources typically associated with schooling contribute significantly to the formation of faith. They are not sufficient, however, to the contemporary task of forming faith. Something more is needed. That something more, I contend, exists in relational practices of the congregation that influence the agency of its formal educational efforts. These patterns of relationality constitute what I am calling the congregation's catechetical culture in and through which faith is both formed and transformed.

The notion of a catechetical culture is obviously linked to practices and traditions we associate with the ancient church practice of catechesis. By linking the notion of catechesis to congregational culture I am suggesting it is something more than a mode of instruction and the congregation is something more than a voluntary association of people held together by common values, beliefs, and practices. The term may seem awkward at first glance, but I have not discovered another metaphor that conveys as well the contextual conditions conducive to forming faith in and through the interplay of a congregation's formal educational structures and informal educational patterns.

My understanding of its significance for contemporary congregations builds on an image in Thomas Groome's discussion of the meaning and history of catechesis.[1] The word, he reminds us, comes from the Greek verb *katéchein*, which means "to resound," "to echo," or "to hand down." In the life of the early church it referred to a pattern of oral instruction emphasizing the accurate transmission of an explanation to some basic teaching. Groome calls it a process of "oral reechoing." His image of "reechoing" caught my attention. It highlights the repetitive interaction of the generations "handing down" some theological idea, value, or practice. We see its form in the repetitive rehearsal of questions and answers in Luther's *Small Cathechism* in each new generation of catechumens. The pattern of listening, questioning, and affirming reinforced by memorizing from generation to generation is set in its first section on the Ten Commandments.

---

1. Groome, *Christian Religious Education*, 6–7.

The First Commandment
Thou shalt have no other Gods.

What does this mean?
We should fear, love, and trust in God above all things.[2]

Similar patterns of instruction introduced children and youth to the content of the Bible in many mainline Protestant congregations during much of the nineteenth and early twentieth centuries. The repetitive patterns through the generations in this catechetical process, however, are not limited to the verbal and cognitive dimensions of faith formation or to the practices of memorizing and explaining. They are also to be found in family and congregational practices of forming habits of prayer, hospitality, and compassion. In their repetition, sounds and shapes, feelings, thoughts, and behaviors associated with these instructional moments reverberate or "re-echo" through the generations. In their reverberations we encounter the faith of ancestors "living still" (as the hymn writer put it) and anticipate the faith of still unknown descendants in the rhythms of our heartbeats, the exercise of our imaginations, and the engagement of our commitments in spontaneous and routine expressions of compassion, love, and justice.

I am reminded of hiking through small canyons near where I live, hearing my voice echoing off the walls, once, twice, and sometimes three or more times. Each hearing reinforces in my memory the sound of my voice, and intensifies in my speaking the experience of my hearing. I would not have heard the echoing of my voice if I had not been surrounded by those canyon walls. The reverberations of the echo required their presence. Something similar to that echo chamber is also required in the education of a congregation if its values, hopes, images, stories, interpretations, and practices of faith are to reverberate from generation to generation. It exists with special force, I contend, in the lively interdependence of three congregational practices. Together they establish important contextual conditions in the catechetical culture of congregations in forming the knowledge and conduct of faith of their members across the generations.

- The practice of *hospitality* creates the conditions for generously including young people into a congregation's life and mission,[3] while subverting at the same time their all too human proclivity to associate predominantly with others of their own kind.

2. *Luther's Small Catechism,* http://www.cph.org.

3. This theme is developed at length in Joyce Mercer's important ethnographic study of children in congregations, published as *Welcoming Children.*

- The practice of *celebration* establishes the curricular framework of a congregation's education by centering the faith journeys of young people on inherited and contemporary encounters with the grace of God in the midst of the realities of human need, struggle, and pain.

- The practice of *conversation* in a congregation cultivates learning that forms faith across the generations as together children, youth, and adults prepare for and participate in the events that give rise to and shape its identity as a community of faith.

The Practice of Hospitality

Several years ago I had the privilege of sharing in the life of a congregation with almost equal numbers of black and white members. I once asked several of those members what distinguished their life together. I asked the question aware that the ancestors of some white folks in the room had helped establish the congregation in the 1820s and "owned" the slaves who sat in the back of the church and were buried in the "colored" section of the church cemetery. I also knew most black families in the congregation had been unwillingly uprooted from their homes in the city by urban renewal and highway projects.[4]

Beside me sat a young African American man. The first to respond to my question, he turned in his seat, pointed his finger at me and declared, "It's because we eat in each other's homes all the time." Others readily concurred. Over the next several weeks I discovered both the accuracy and significance of his words. Black and white church members not only ate in each other's homes "all the time," they joined each other on Sundays before worship in the church kitchen for a cup of coffee. Most everyone, children, youth, and adults, participated in the monthly potluck suppers in the church gymnasium, and on the first Sunday of the month the whole congregation gathered at the communion rail. When the pastor welcomed folks to worship and other public gatherings, she made clear the "table" was set for everyone: "We are family here. We want you to feel at home in this place."

It soon became apparent to us that eating together provided opportunities for talking with each other, something they did in many other settings as well: for thirty minutes to an hour on the lawn after worship, during

4. For an extended description of this congregation see Foster and Brelsford, *We Are the Church Together*, 41ff.

weekly work parties to mow the lawn and clean the church building, during the annual retreats and night-long vigils over the biannual church barbecue, while sitting together to cheer their high school youth at football and basketball games, and before, during, and after congregational and neighborhood meetings. Their conversations seemed to reinforce the enjoyment they experienced in their life together. They provided opportunities for sharing little victories over the racism they encountered in themselves, the community, and among their denominational leaders, and for discussing the pastor's sermons and the congregation's various ministries.

We were intrigued by the extent to which the congregation's children and youth moved in and out of these conversations with a remarkable lack of self-consciousness. Sometimes they listened in. Other times they freely interjected thoughts and opinions about the topic at hand. Most Sundays one of the children stood with a greeter at the door welcoming those entering the church. Children and youth assumed active roles of leadership in worship. They participated with adults in weekly work parties to clean the church and maintain the grounds. They helped with the set-up of the monthly potluck suppers. They added their voices to congregational deliberations over local church and community issues. We soon discovered that a relatively new stained glass window depicting Jesus surrounded by children had been an intentional choice. It declared that in this place, young people were welcome.

The practice of hospitality is not easy. Despite biblical injunctions to the effect that strangers bear God's gifts, through most of Christian history congregations have generally been more open to people like themselves and suspicious of strangers. Congregations are typically more interested in stability and homogeneity than in the flexibility, adaptability, and even transformation the presence of strangers often requires. We need only think of the impact a new baby has on a household or of the challenges to our settled ways when a grandparent moves into the house. These "strangers," no matter how expected or loved, still disrupt familiar routines and lead to new family patterns. Even when we embrace the idea, how much more disruptive to our views of ourselves and the world when someone from a different culture, race, religious tradition, political perspective, or economic experience moves next door to us! Or joins our congregation!

Since we live in an era in which generational differences are not only emphasized but often intensified in popular culture, the presence of young people can be equally disruptive to adult expectations and decorum. Babies cry. Toddlers squirm. The attention of children wanders. Teenagers challenge dress codes and quickly identify hypocrisies they see in us. They are easily bored and we are distracted.

The tension we feel when distracted by the presence of young people often originates, as Joyce Mercer observes, in our ambivalence over the multiple messages we and young people send to each other. Mercer's concern is with the contrariety that often exists in the differences of our developmental, cultural, and personal perceptions and the range of our responses to some shared event or experience.[5] As adults we often seek to accommodate the contrary messages we receive from young people by suppressing our reactions to their words and actions. We act as if we do not see or hear them. They become invisible to us. We are just as likely to require them to suppress their thoughts and actions and to act as if they were the adults they are not.

A more common strategy for dealing with the messages we do not understand or appreciate from young people in our congregations, however, is to create alternative and supposedly more congenial places for them so their presence will not disturb us and we will not constrain them. We isolate them in learning and worship settings and in mission and social activities. Some congregations even build this isolation into the structure of their church buildings by locating infant nurseries and youth rooms as far from the sanctuary of the church or classrooms for adults as possible. I experienced something different in the congregation described above.

The members of this congregation assumed all adults were responsible for the safety and well-being of all the children. When a child did something well, that child received the affirmation of adults from across the congregation. When a child acted up, the child was confronted, and if necessary, reprimanded by the adult who was closest. When a child spoke up in a meeting or at the table during a potluck meal adults typically took note, often building on or weaving that child's contribution into something they might say later. The patterns of mutuality across the generations in this congregation, I gradually realized, shifts the recent concern for the safety of children and youth in churches and schools across the nation from the regulatory guidelines of "safe sanctuary" policies to the creation of a culture of safety in which the whole congregation is accountable for the care and well-being of its children and youth.

From this perspective the practice of hospitality not only creates a welcoming environment, it cultivates the mutuality and interdependence

5. Mercer, *Welcoming Children*, 118ff.

of the generations. The affirmation of the maturity integral to the capacities and abilities of children and youth as they move from infancy into childhood and then into adolescence anticipates the affirmation of the childlikeness that gives rise to trust and hope in the faith of adults. This insight was reinforced for me one Sunday morning after the pastor had led the congregation in the prayer of confession. Apparently relationships in the congregation had been sorely tested the previous week. So she encouraged everyone of every age to stand and greet "each other with the words, 'In the name of Christ you are forgiven.'"[6] Children, youth, and adults from different racial, cultural, and socio-economic backgrounds stood up and began to move around the sanctuary of that congregation, taking hold of each other's hands, looking each other in the eye, and pronouncing these profound words of absolution. Adults sought out young people. Young people spoke words of forgiveness to adults. In the freedom of this hospitable environment, the young people of this congregation became agents of gospel. That should be the goal of every congregation's faith-forming education.

This observation brings us to a second practice in the catechetical cultures of congregation. This practice directs our attention to the curriculum of faith formation embedded in the structure of a congregation's significant events.

Practices of Celebration

The adaptive challenge of educating for faith involves a shift in how we think about the structures in and through which faith is formed. For most of their recent history mainline Protestant denominations have assumed the school with its age group classes, designated teachers, prepared curriculum resources, and formal classroom spaces for teaching and learning provided the primary structural context for faith formation. For decades the school functioned effectively in that role when its efforts were supported and reinforced by other agencies and forces in the church and larger culture. With the collapse of these supporting and reinforcing agencies, however, an alternative structural framework for the formation of the faith of children and youth is needed. That alternative framework, however, does not need to be created. It already exists in the potential of a congregation's celebrative events to establish the curricular structure for the formation of its members' faith.

6. Foster and Brelsford, *We Are the Church Together*, 55–56.

A clue to the formative possibilities in this framework can be found in the ways children learn to celebrate their birthdays. They learn the traditions, songs, ritual actions, and expectations for their attitudes and behavior by participating in birthdays. The same thing can be said about the experience of a group of children who told their pastor that communion was their favorite part of church. In a sense that should not be surprising. In this congregation they had been welcomed to the table for as long as they could remember. Birthdays and communion in their experience had much in common. Each includes a set of actions repeated over and over again. With time that repetition forms habits that carry expectations for our participation from one moment of celebration into the next. Through that repetition we become increasingly confident in our knowledge of expectations for our participation and competent in the performance of those expectations. For these children communion occurred on the first Sunday of the month. It was something they could both look forward to and depend on. They enjoyed the experience of gathering around the communion table with the rest of the congregation. They especially liked the hymn that always concluded the liturgy in this congregation's worship. It was the favorite of several children and most knew it by memory. Albert Borgmann, a philosopher of science, has suggested why this event may have become so important to them. Celebration, he notes, "constitutes the concrete and hopeful center of communal life."[7] That is certainly how most children view their birthdays, and the children in this congregation seemed to view communion.

Elsewhere I have noted that as we participate in the celebration of the events that distinguish the common life of a congregation we begin to identify with its perspectives and values.[8] We begin to take on its character. We begin to view the world through meanings and practices it emphasizes. We discover, in the process, clues for relating to others and the world around us. That center of our communal life, however, has been diminished in our modern world by the dominance of our commitments to technologies of production and consumption in the spheres of our public or common life, including the public spaces of our congregations in which we gather.

We can see the thrust of this insight in the marketing of a new film. It has all the pedagogical marks associated with celebration. Advertisements, promotions, advance reviews, and CDs of the musical score are released

---

7. Borgmann, *Power Failure*, 37.

8. See Foster, *Educating Congregations*, 37–50, for an earlier discussion of the function of events in the education of congregations.

well ahead of the first showing of the film. This "pedagogical activity" unleashes a torrent of "learning" as our growing familiarity with its genre, its technologies, and its themes heighten our anticipation of participating in the event of its showing. The effectiveness of this marketing educational process was dramatized for me by a colleague whose daughters were not allowed to see a certain major film aimed at children, but who nevertheless had learned all the songs from the film by memory from their friends.

The impact of the technologies of production and consumption is as strong in our churches. One only has to observe how marketing strategies dominate educational values in the production and use of curriculum resources in much congregational education. Especially in congregations caught up in so-called "rotation models" of teaching and learning, the result can rarely be little more than the production of activities for religious entertainment (Borgmann's term) or religious "enrichment" (mine).[9] Borgmann argues that celebrations countering the technological dominance of our contemporary communities must be grounded, instead, in the concrete and specific things that make up our daily experience. This is not a new insight for Christians whose celebrations focus on such everyday things as water, bread, wine, marrying, baptizing, illness, dying, taking up a vocation, and responding to injustice or pain. In these things that matter, Borgmann emphasizes, "people do not just play at something, but in playing are definite persons, where they do not just take up some role on some stage, but are fully engaged in this, their own place, and where they do not just send and receive messages in some fashionable code, but encounter one another in the depths of their being."[10] Communal celebrations, in other words, do "not arise from abstract designs," they are rooted in "the reality of the public space" of the home, congregation, or community in which they occur. From this perspective the place or setting of a community's celebration and the "sacramental dignity" of concrete things and practices like bread and wine, water and friendship, prayer, and acts of justice and reconciliation are intertwined and inform each other. They become the impetus to the "joyful engagement with the physical presence and radiance" embedded in the act or practice of celebrating.[11]

The structure embedded in celebrating the concrete events of congregational life is a simple one. It begins with *preparing* people to participate

9. Borgmann, *Power Failure*, 37; Foster, *Educating Congregations*, 28.

10. Borgmann, *Power Failure*, 50.

11. Ibid., 50–55.

in them, preferably in age-appropriate ways that honor our developmental patterns of learning. This is a crucial step in our modern era because congregational leaders can no longer assume those who might participate in any celebrative event will have the knowledge or skill to do so. It continues with the act of *participation* in the event itself and concludes with the *recollection and critique* of that experience to discern and respond to claims it may have on our lives.

Each step in this repetitive pedagogical process has the potential of being a catalyst to the conversations and interactions in the congregation that sustain and renew the curricular content of the event embedded in its repetitive practice. Like a rock thrown into a pond, the accumulative impact of these three educational components of an event ripple out across a congregation in ways that no one can order or control. As we anticipate the experience of the event and then participate in it, we align ourselves with its meanings and possibilities. As we accede to its demands for participation in the event, we begin to incorporate its claims on our thinking and doing. As we begin to identify with those demands we may become increasingly open to the experience of others and to scholarly insights about their meaning, significance, and relevance for our lives.

The cluster of events associated with Christmas provides a good example. If a congregation takes the celebration of this event seriously, certain hymns are practiced in formal and informal settings repeatedly as an integral part of the preparatory season of Advent. Over time *Silent Night, Away in a Manger,* and *O Little Town of Bethlehem* become associated with the celebration of the season through the repetition of the season. As they are repeated in each season and from season to season children develop enough familiarity with their words and tunes that they can sing them from memory. Their rhythms and meanings become embedded in their relationship to the season. As the years go by their repertoire of music associated with the celebration expands. Its sounds and rhythms enhance their anticipation of the season. The texts convey images and meanings that over time become identified with Christmas. Eventually the carols of Advent and Christmas contribute to a framework of meaning through which children will hear and respond to sermons, discussions of the birth narratives in the Gospels, interpretations of contemporary gift giving, and calls for service and justice in their communities.

Preparing for the celebration of Christmas, however, involves more than becoming familiar with its music. I am reminded of a pastor who wanted school-age children (and many adults) to discover there are many ways of seeing and understanding the birth of Christ. There are many ways to approach the celebration of that birth. He chose to make use of the children's moments that were part of the liturgy in his congregation's worship to compare and contrast different expectations for that event in the Matthew and Luke versions of the story. So through the season of Advent he wondered with the children why Matthew might emphasize the visit of wise men and Luke the visit of shepherds. He shared some of his own questions: why do we think there were three wise men when the Bible does not tell us how many there were? Where did the notion of three wise men come from? Why don't the Gospels of Mark and John have anything to say about the birth of Jesus?

The information he shared with the children may have been new both to them and the adults and youth overhearing them. It probably would not take hold of their imaginations, however, until it had spilled over into the conversations of families and among the members of the congregation. It would probably not be remembered long if it were not discussed often enough to challenge the hold on their memories of the more synthetic versions of the story. This takes time; indeed, it may take years. That is one reason why events celebrating the creative and redemptive activity of God must be repeated over and again. Even then, their influence in forming the faith of children and youth is limited if they do not permeate the informal conversations of their congregations. This is a third practice we find in the catechetical cultures of congregations.

The Practice of Congregational Conversation

The practice of congregational conversation originates in what James Carse refers to as the "exuberant orality" in all religions and a distinctive feature of Jewish and Christian religious traditions.[12] The ancient biblical writers envisioned God calling all creation into existence through speech. The prophets over and again introduced God's intentions with the phrase "Thus *says* the Lord." The Gospel of John portrays the renewal of God's intent for our existence through the *Word made flesh* in Jesus Christ. The ministry of Jesus continues to have power for us because his followers remembered his words and passed them along to others.

The process of the speaking that calls us into life is not unfamiliar to us. It is replicated over and again in the experience of parents and most

---

12. Carse, *The Religious Case Against Belief*, 154.

often among mothers of newborn children. Holding their children on their laps so they are facing each other, they draw their babies' attention to their mouths with sounds and words. In the repetition of this developmentally appropriate *practice* those babies soon begin to speak back as they strive to imitate the sounds they hear. In their responses to their mother's encouraging words, they are called into the speech of the families and communities into which they were born. In the repetitious "reechoing" of this verbal interaction they are immersed in and take on ways of perceiving and thinking identified with being French, Chinese, Spanish, English, or Zulu as well as Jewish, Hindu, or Christian, as well as Methodist, Orthodox, or Pentecostal, and even as participants in specific communities of faith known as First, Grace, or St. Paul churches.

The relationships that constitute our communities, in other words, originate in and are nurtured and sustained by our practices of communicating with each other. This means the quality and character of the informal conversations in our congregations make a difference in forming the faith of our children and youth. A friend once told me he always looked forward to the conversations of a congregation after its worship had concluded. The length of time folks stayed around to talk and the candor of the connections they made between their experience of worship and the circumstances of their lives provided this friend with significant clues to the vitality and depth of their shared life and ministry. I recalled the wisdom in his comment while visiting the congregation in which its black and white members ate in each other's homes "all the time."

That congregation's pastor was a constant catalyst to conversation. Daily she jogged through the neighborhood, running around the high school track while the athletic teams were practicing and inevitably engaging youth and coaches in brief conversations. Her jogging through the neighborhood included brief stops at each of the shops in a local strip mall to talk briefly with the business owners. She consistently arrived early for meetings and fellowship dinners to engage other early arrivals in conversation. It did not take long before more and more people were also arriving early with the intention of "helping" set up whatever was to follow, but spending most of their time talking with each other. When someone in the congregation had an idea the pastor invariably suggested it be discussed with someone who might have a different view of the idea to see what he or she thought. It did not take long in her ministry in that congregation before most issues and proposals had been thoroughly discussed by members before and after worship, over the phone, and during neighborhood meetings long before they reached the committee meeting agenda. It often took a long time until some controversial issue was ready for the formal conversation of a committee or board meeting. When black and white members in the congregation crossed each other, she again invariably urged them to "talk it out." Nowhere was the impact of the conversations in this congregation more powerful than on the women's retreat when black and white women "let down their hair" to talk about what most deeply mattered to them late into the night, or during the biannual barbecue when black and white men tending the fire also spent the night discussing local sports events before sharing with each other some of their deepest faith and life issues.

The function and structure of conversations like these that hold, sustain, and renew the shared life of human communities have increasingly intrigued a number of scholars.[13] Walter Brueggemann was among the first to catch my attention in an essay exploring the need among people of faith for a "communal language" for talking among themselves and a "public language" for talking with people who did not share their assumptions and values.[14] Drawing on the story of the confrontation of the people of Jerusalem with the Assyrian army at its gate in 2 Kings 18:17–27, he highlights the necessity for the Jews "behind the wall" of the city to consider their situation in their own language before speaking in the public language of international discourse with their enemies, the Assyrians, "at the wall." Brueggemann did not describe in this essay what an education looked like that prepared people of faith across the generations to converse either "behind the wall" among themselves or in public "at the wall."

During the time we spent in several racially diverse congregations like the one described above, however, we began to have some sense of what a bilingual faith-forming educational strategy might look like. As members of this congregation and others like it talked with each other in their homes and at church behind or inside the walls of their common life, they practiced ways of talking with people in the larger community who were often either challenged or offended by the life of faith they were creating together. In their practice they engaged as they modeled for the young people in their midst expectations for their participation in those conversations. As those young people began to contribute to those conversations, adult members

13. Cf. Brueggemann, "The Legitimacy of a Sectarian Hermeneutic: 2 Kings 18–19," in *Education for Citizenship and Discipleship*, 3–34; see also Tracy, *Plurality and Ambiguity*; Chopp, *The Power to Speak* for a theological perspective; and Purnell, *Conversation as Ministry* for an exploration of the practice of conversation in theology and ministry.

14. Brueggemann, "The Legitimacy of a Sectarian Hermeneutic," 5–6.

of the congregation drew them into their practice and encouraged their participation.

The challenges of cultivating the language of faith for speaking both behind and at the wall have become more difficult in recent years. The modes and means of our communication have proliferated. We continue to talk face to face but often only on occasion. Some of us still correspond with each other by mail. The Internet, however, has almost rendered our letter-writing obsolete. The telephone long ago made it possible to talk with others without seeing them. With new technologies we now text or Twitter, use Skype, and Facebook. We tend, unfortunately, to confuse our chatter with talking or communicating. The challenge for those of us who are older, moreover, is that young people are more adept in using these new communication strategies than we are. This gap, as some call it, intensifies the difficulties we experience in communicating across the generations. With the continuing introduction of new communication technologies, we face the possibility of having to relearn over and again how to communicate with each other. Who knows how we will be communicating with each other in the future? Who knows to what extent these future modes of communication will diminish or enhance the modeling of our faith conversations across the generations? Who knows to what extent they will support and sustain our quest to gather our children and youth into the exuberant orality of our faith traditions?

These challenges for communities of faith envisioning their future through their children are real. A number of these newer technologies already blur distinctions between our private and public languages. They obscure differences among the languages of different communities of faith as well as with the languages of those who do not identify with or relate to any faith tradition. David Denby, in a critical review of the 2010 movie *The Social Network,* about the origins of Facebook, makes the point. Facebook, as one example of these new technologies, he argues, is a paradox. It "celebrates the aura of intimacy . . . while providing the relief of distance, substituting bodiless sharing and the thrills of self-created celebrityhood for close encounters of the first kind." He continues by observing that "Karl Marx suggested that, in the capitalist age, we began to treat one another as commodities. *The Social Network* suggests we now treat one another as packets of information."[15]

---

15. Denby, "Influencing People: David Fincher and the 'The Social Network,'" 99.

Jaron Lanier, who has been described as the "father of virtual reality technology," goes a step further. He points out that "Communication is now often experienced as a superhuman phenomenon that towers above individuals. A new generation has come of age with a reduced expectation of what a person can be, and of who each person might become."[16] He asserts further that in this situation the empathy giving life to our communicating with each other in conversation is lost. Sherry Turkle, Professor of the Social Studies of Science and Technology at the Massachusetts Institute of Technology, underscores Lanier's observation: the networked life we now experience through these new technologies "allows us to hide from each other, even as we are tethered to each other." In this new cultural context many young people would "rather text than talk."[17]

Accounting for the current and future influence of these technological innovations in the conversations of our congregations about the creative and redemptive activity of God in the education of our children and youth is a profound challenge. If we do not embrace that challenge we may well subvert possibilities for a deep and robust faith among our children and youth. I contend a deeper understanding of the role and shape of a congregation's conversation in the midst of this technological revolution in the formation of faith is needed. Especially important to that understanding is an appreciation for the relational and consensual dynamics in conversations that sustain and renew the celebration of events centering a congregation's catechetical culture.

Congregational Conversation in Faith Forming Education is Relational. Conversation involves more than the exchange of words. Conversation is a relational practice. But it is not just any type of relationship. Conversation draws us into the company of others. It does more. It establishes patterns of reciprocity that draw us into possibilities of intimacy. We often describe that intimacy as companionship. The interdependence and mutuality of companionship is sustained over time in the continuity of our verbal and non-verbal exchanges with each other. Through these exchanges we participate in the mutuality of influencing and being influenced, of shaping and being shaped, of forming and being formed, of freeing ourselves from and binding ourselves to each other and the things we value in common. The pattern is set in the "communication" of parents with their very young children. It is expanded in the "communication" of young people with peers

16. Lanier, *You Are Not a Gadget*, 4.

17. Turkle, *Alone Together*, 1.

and a growing circle of adults that includes, among others, their parents, teachers, coaches, and mentors.

Conversation as a basic feature of these exchanges is not a neutral activity. It involves more than the transfer of information, observations, or opinions. It invites and resists. It risks and negotiates. It reveals and hides. This is as true of the conversations among children as it is of the conversations between children, youth, and adults. It anticipates openness to change and being changed. In face-to-face conversation non-verbal cues conveyed through eye-contact, body posture, and tone of voice provide revelatory clues to the intent or meaning embedded in the words we speak or use. When speaking over the phone in the absence of these clues we give increased attention to tone of voice and choice of words for clues to the intentions and meanings in the words of our conversation partners. In the written conversation of our letters and email messages our attention is focused even more closely on clues to self-disclosing phrases, images, and metaphors.

This suggests that through the relational interactivity of conversation we may become something other than what we once were. We may be called into new activity and new modes of being. In this regard conversation can be life changing. Again this may be as true for children as for adults. It can enhance even as it can also diminish the educational intentions of a community. It is therefore always political, engaging us in the exercise of exerting and responding to the power dynamics embedded in the patterns of our mutual interaction. Conversation can consequently be contrasted with the imposition of authoritarian messages and the chatter of "information packets" conveyed through text-messages and twittering. Both forms of communication eliminate many of the cues we need to ascertain the intentions or meanings in the exchange of our words and actions.

Congregational Conversation in Faith Forming Education Is Consensual. Congregational or community conversation that cultivates the formation and transformation of faith is necessarily consensual. This is a critical issue for congregations seeking to embrace the range of the diversity to be found in them. It depends on at least two things: agreement about who is to be included in the conversation and shared expectations for the confluence of meanings children, youth, and adults bring to their efforts to communicate with each other. There is little or no conversation when the words we speak are simply directed at another person or group. Instead it requires some openness to embracing the fullness of the humanity of the other. For those of us who understand our humanity in our relationship with God it involves, as well, a keen sense of that relatedness.

In his discussion of what it means to love our neighbor, theologian Miroslav Volf draws our attention to the drama embedded in the movements of embracing each other. They include "opening the arms, waiting, closing the arms, and opening them again" to release each other in full recognition of the reciprocity of our connectedness and our distinctiveness.[18] The drama of embrace embedded in conversation involves similar moves: suspending judgment as we open ourselves to the possibility of becoming vulnerable to each other and then waiting to see if the other responds with a degree of corresponding openness and vulnerability. If we sense some possibility of openness, the sense of mutuality we experience in the exchange of our verbal and non-verbal messages is intensified. We sense we are in some way at one with the other. We then celebrate the uniqueness of each other in some act of leave-taking.

Often in our relationship with young children these moves come naturally. We respond freely and without hesitancy to their spontaneous hugs. For the child our responsiveness to the open spontaneity of these hugs becomes a building block to the trust Erik Erikson argued was the foundation for the rest of the development of our sense of well-being. Erikson, however, also noted that the capacity for trusting we may learn as young children must be re-learned over and again as we negotiate each of the developmental learning tasks associated with growing older.

The mutuality of companionship embedded in the conversation drama among adults or among children, youth, and adults, in other words, involves more than agreement over the meaning of words. It has to do as well, with the confluence of values, perspectives, and sensibilities in shared rhythms, metaphors, images, and patterns of "reechoing" in our speaking and listening. Together, they create a sense of being at one with each other, even when we encounter in each other differences in our opinions and beliefs. Perhaps the apostle Paul's comparison of the church to the interconnectedness of the human body[19] most effectively conveys the deep sense of mutuality and interdependence we powerfully experience in consensual conversation.

The experience itself may be hard to define, but again, no matter what our age, we certainly recognize its power when the words of others silence

18. Volf, *Exclusion and Embrace*, 141.

19. 1 Cor 12:12.

or marginalize us, when the words we hear sound familiar but the meanings attached to them escape us, when we miss the humor in jokes being told, whenever we stumble over the patterns and rhythms of the verbal interaction, or find ourselves victimized or oppressed by them. We may be less aware of its characteristics when we find ourselves experiencing the intimacy of companionship or the intensity of mutuality in the spontaneity of our interactions with each other. We may be even less prone to recognize its features in the mutuality of our candor.

When conversation is consensual our interactions with each other convey a deep sense of civility. Stephen Carter defines civility as "the sum of the many sacrifices we are called to make for the sake of living together."[20] This suggests that "To be civilized is to understand that we live in society as in a household, and that within that household, if we are to be moral people, our relationships with other people . . . are governed by standards of behavior that limit our freedom. Our duty to follow those standards does not depend on whether or not we happen to agree with or even like each other."[21] Nor does it depend on some achievement of maturity. Rather, as James Carse argues, it "evolves spontaneously" out of our desire "to get to the bottom of the very mystery" that brings us together. Carse describes this experience as *communitas*. It relies on the stability grounded in the civility of a group or organization, even as it transcends and may renew it.[22] The catechetical culture of a congregation, in other words, requires the interdependence of *civility* and *communitas* in faith-forming education.

Civility creates the conditions for the respect that Christians have traditionally associated with being neighbors of one another. This relationship, first modeled in the relationship God seeks with us, is given form in the covenantal bonds we have with God and consequently, with neighbors. Respect from inside this relationship requires empathy or the ability to listen from inside the perspective of the other with enough humility to see in one's own perspective both deficiencies and new possibilities. Empathy gives rise to *communitas*.

The Christian story is filled with examples. We see it in the transformation of the consciousness of the disciples when Jesus invited the children in the crowd to join him. We see it in the overflowing generosity and compassion of the father of the prodigal son that culminates in the restoration,

20. Carter, *Civility: Manners, Morals, and the Etiquette of Democracy*, 11.

21. Ibid., 15.

22. Carse, *The Religious Case Against Belief*, 84–85.

indeed, the transformation of their relationship. It is evident in the experience of two men on the road to Emmaus reflecting back on their *conversation* with the stranger who had joined them: "Were not our hearts burning within us while he was talking to us on the road, while he was opening the scriptures to us?"[23] Centuries later we too may experience a similar sense of "burning" in our hearts in the midst of conversations that similarly call us, no matter what our age or circumstance, into some deeper and more profound encounter with the creative and redemptive "words" of God in and through each other.

A Congregation's Conversation Sustains the Curricular Infrastructure of its Catechetical Culture. When suggesting that a congregation's conversation is a basic feature in its curricular "infrastructure," I have in mind the interactive communication patterns in families, groups, and organizations that form and sustain its deepest values, perspectives, and practices. Although the term itself may be unfamiliar, the notion should not be strange to Christian communities that understand themselves living in response to the call of God to be agents of that call in the world. In a sense, one could say we are who we are because we communicate. This theme runs through Edward T. Hall's study of the verbal and non-verbal cultural vocabularies of many different peoples around the world.[24] In every culture he studied, he discovered three patterns in their communication with each other. He simply identified them as their informal, formal, and technical vocabularies. Together these vocabularies create the curricular infrastructure for our interpersonal, social-cultural, and institutional efforts to transmit the values, commitments, and practices we cherish on to our children.

The vocabulary of *informal* conversation is situational and imprecise. It establishes predispositions to mutuality, gives momentum to the rhythms of our interactions with each other, and creates a contextual framework for hearing into the intent of our speaking. It dominates our verbal interactions with our children. It gathers us into common linguistic experiences that frame and channel our messages to each other. It makes use of stories, jokes, confessions, commentaries, and moments of formal and didactic instruction. The intent and meaning of its messages are intensified by non-verbal cues children learn primarily through trial and error in their interactions with family, peers, and community members. Critiques of informal

---

23. Luke 24:32.

24. Hall, *The Silent Language*, 66ff.

messages tend to rely on personal authority or the authority of a primary reference group.

Until the 1960s at least, the sources and catalysts to the informal religious vocabulary in the conversations of most American mainline Protestants existed primarily in the interplay of congregational and denominational life that cut across their ideological lines. People were not necessarily aware of differences in the Gospel accounts of the birth of Christ or of the two accounts of creation in the book of Genesis, but their basic encounters with the confluence of stories like these provided a common framework for hearing sermons, participating in Bible study groups, commenting on political events, and making ethical or moral decisions across the distinctions of their denominational differences. In similar fashion, the Baltimore Catechism and the language of faith embedded in the rhythm of the liturgy and other rituals fulfilled a similar function for the more formal teaching and learning in Roman Catholic parishes. Denominational tradition, racial and cultural heritage, social or economic class, geographic region, and local circumstances contributed to what might well be called the dialects of faith among Christians in the nation. These denominational dialects provided congregations with a *formal* vocabulary, to use Hall's term, that helped their members distinguish communities and faith traditions from each other.

The formal vocabulary of a congregation's faith tradition, in other words, is a primary source for the content of the informal vocabularies in the conversations of a congregation's members. It provides a shared framework of meaning for the interpretation of biblical narratives, hymns, creeds, and community practices. As such it functions as a controlling tradition linking and reinforcing the affirmations and practices of a congregation with those of its denominational or religious heritage. In the recent past the formal vocabulary of Christian faith was typically identified with "the lesson" in the Sunday schools of many Protestant congregations and the "right answers" of the catechism in many Catholic, Lutheran, and Episcopal congregations. In both instances familiarity with their vocabularies of faith was viewed as a prerequisite for full participation in the congregations of their respective religious traditions. Whether or not they were useful in the discourse of a congregation or parish depended, however, on the extent to which they energized their informal conversations.

Hall also noted that communities draw on the *technical vocabularies* of specialists in their conversations. In religious communities those specialists include biblical scholars, theologians, ethicists, historians, and the scholars of the practices of ministry. It also includes congregational leaders, denominational staff, and the entrepreneurial consultants who mediate the technical language of the specialists in the formal and informal vocabularies of local communities of faith. The technical vocabulary of Christian communities is used in Bible commentaries, scholarly interpretations of theology, analyses of historical, social, and ethical movements and figures, theoretical works in homiletics, pastoral care, and religious education, as well as in the constitutions and polity handbooks of denominations and congregations. Just as the informal conversations of a congregation or religious tradition may become catalysts to the deliberations of formal conversations or the research that energizes technical conversations, so the continuing vitality of our informal conversations requires continuing engagement with the content of the technical conversations in the congregation's religious tradition. These technical conversations are especially important in revitalizing the relevance of a congregation's faith tradition in the midst of the influence of its changing situation and circumstances.

The isolation of any of these vocabularies in the conversations of a congregation can only diminish their individual vitality and reify their meaning and significance. This insight was reinforced for me by conversations with two pastors in two different old mainline Protestant denominations while working on this chapter. One is the pastor of a congregation in a small town in the American west dependent on an agricultural economy. The other is pastor of a southern U.S. small city downtown church. The first pastor described for me a moment from a class of senior high youth she was teaching. As they were working their way through a curriculum unit exploring the biblical narratives of creation, two "very bright" young women said "they believed the world was created exactly like it said in the Bible." When encouraged to explain what they meant, they had little to say other than that they "didn't believe in evolution." Aware that the parents of these girls and many other leaders of this congregation held a more nuanced view of the relation of the biblical story to theories of evolution, she asked them if they had ever discussed the topic with their parents. They had not. Neither did they remember ever hearing a discussion on evolution and creation in their Sunday school classes or youth group meetings. Rather, they just knew "evolution" was false because their friends "had told them so." Moreover, they had little interest in any other point of view. In this instance at least, little or no informal conversation existed in that congregation about the relationship of science and the biblical accounts of creation. Neither were the formal and technical vocabularies that had informed the faith of their parents vital enough to nuance the influence of the informal conversations of their peers at school about the messages on the subject they were hearing.

The second pastor shared a similar story about the disparity between the formal vocabularies of faith in the congregation he serves and the impact of the media-influenced informal conversations among its youth. The curriculum unit in the confirmation class he was teaching had been organized around the theme of "loving God with heart, soul, strength, and mind." He then described a session in which "we talked about loving God, self, neighbor, and enemy. These kids—good kids," he emphasized, "had grown up in the church" but they did not "believe love can be stronger than violence." Beneath that belief lurked the conviction that the love of God was inevitably limited and a faith in the possibilities of that love claimed by their congregation was a sham. Both pastors then describe the absence of lively informal and sustained formal conversations adequate to the task of forming the faith of their children and youth bombarded with alternative stories competing for their attention and loyalty.

So how do pastors and teachers create conditions for the conversations that help reinforce and sustain the remembering crucial to the tasks of maintaining, deepening, and renewing both personal and corporate faith? The answer begins by acknowledging that traditional patterns for congregational governance are no longer adequate to the task of holding in community the diversity of groups and experience often found in them. In both parish and voluntary forms of congregational life over the past one hundred years, more and more substructures have been instituted to respond to the growing consciousness of folk to the differences of people in the congregation: women's and men's groups, youth groups, classes for persons of different ages and abilities, experiences for people at different points of their faith journeys, and a wide variety of activities designed to accommodate the range of interests children, youth, and adults bring to these varied programmatic options.

More recently, congregations have also sought to accommodate the growing social, racial, cultural, economic, and theological diversity among the people they serve. This has led to interest-based educational activities for children, worship in a variety of styles, self-help and dependency groups, advocacy programs, and an ever wider array of social services. While responsive to the interests and sometimes the needs of persons, each new group also separates and often isolates people from each other and, in the process, diminishes the depth and quality of the conversations that should hold everything together. Although each of these groups can be considered to be important to the life of a congregation, they also can subvert the potential for the coherence of a congregation's informal faith vocabulary. This lack of coherence becomes evident both in the absence of lively informal conversation about matters of faith and in the chatter that often substitutes for conversation in the interactions of many congregations.

Once in a while the media highlights the story of some congregation in which its diversity becomes unbearable as it considers some political, social, ethical issue, or theological question. Rarely do we hear on those same news reports stories of people leaving congregations because they no longer feel they are participating in some shared mission or purpose attuned to the initiative of God. And yet, as I talk with people who are active in some congregation and others who have left, they all typically express a deep desire to be part of a cohering and meaningful faith community. If a consciousness of pluralism is indeed a prevailing characteristic of contemporary life as some scholars have claimed, the vitality, if not the future, of voluntary or parish congregations is in doubt. So once again, how do congregational leaders nurture the conversations that support and sustain the education of children and youth contributing to their formation as faithful followers of Jesus Christ? With this question we turn our attention to a third task in the challenge congregations face in their quests to educate for faith: namely, the cultivation of an educational imagination with the capacity to envision adaptive leaps and adjustments congregational and denominational leaders might need to make in building up and equipping the future of their congregations through the faith of their children and youth.

Discussion Questions and Exercises for Personal and Group Reflection

1. In what ways is the congregational practice of hospitality for young people a theological practice?

2. What conditions and practices in your congregation convey welcome most clearly to children and to youth?

3. What event in your congregation most effectively includes children and/or youth? Describe in detail their preparation, participation, and opportunities for critical reflection on the event. How does their preparation cultivate their growing skill in using the formal vocabulary

of your congregation's religious tradition in the formal and informal conversations of the congregation?

4. If it is possible to meet with a group of older children or youth in a congregation, ask them the following questions:

   a. Do you feel welcome in this congregation? If so, what is it that most makes you feel welcome?

   b. Who in the congregation do you know best? How wide is the age range of those people?

   c. What events in the life of the congregation do you most anticipate? What do you do to prepare to participate in them? What stories and rituals and songs associated with those events do you most like?

   d. When do you have opportunities to talk with some adult or adults about the life and mission of the church and your place in it?

   e. If possible, share the results of this conversation with others among the leaders of the congregation.

Chapter Five

Educational Imagination in Adaptive Change

*Do not be conformed to this world, but be transformed by the
renewal of your minds that you may discern the will of God—
what is good and acceptable and perfect.*

Romans 12:2

Introduction

The adaptive challenge for congregations in creating catechetical cultures capable of forming the faith of their children requires a lively and ecclesially grounded educational imagination. Attention to that imaginative capacity, however, is woefully missing in contemporary discussions of education in mainline Protestant congregations. Instead, often romanticized memories of a lively past with highly trained professional and volunteer educators, extensive programs of leader development, developmentally appropriate curriculum resources, and well-attended Sunday schools continue to influence expectations for contemporary congregational education. That day is long gone. A new educational imagination, one distinctively shaped in the crucible of a congregation's theological traditions and practices in its new and changing circumstances and conditions, is needed.

120

This ecclesially grounded educational imagination must be capable of re-envisioning the role of catechesis, schooling, curriculum, teaching, and learning in tasks of forming, building up, and equipping congregations as catechetical cultures seeking to live faithfully in a secular and multi-faith world. In that effort it must also reframe the technological orientation in most recent discussions about the future of schooling and challenge the marketing strategies influencing congregational decisions about what to teach and how to learn.[1]

During the past forty years many attempts have been made to revive a lively conversation in churches about education in forming faith. John Westerhoff's vision of religious socialization and James Fowler's study of faith development were particularly influential for a time. Thomas Groome's exploration of "shared praxis" in Christian religious education enlivened Catholic and Protestant discussions of the field and its possibilities. Mary Elizabeth Moore drew our attention to the interplay of theological and educational method, feminist perspectives, and a concern for the environment. Grant Shockley expanded the discussion with insights from the African American religious experience. Anne Streaty Wimberly, Evelyn Parker, Lynne Westfield, Fred Smith, and others continue his project. Richard Osmer and others have argued for the re-articulation of Christian education as an explicitly practical theological enterprise.[2] The Institute for Youth Ministry at Princeton Theological Seminary has been the catalyst to a creative conversation on youth, spirituality, and ministry. The Valparaiso Project on the Education and Formation of People of Faith, through a wide ranging exploration of Christian practices, has touched the lives of many pastors and congregations. A number of folk have gathered around issues related to the spirituality of children, formation in Jewish and Christian traditions, and the development of innovative pedagogical strategies and curriculum resources. The latter includes, but is not limited to Jerome Berryman's *Godly Play*, Wynn McGregor's *The Way of the Child*, and a popular pedagogical strategy called "rotation." They have produced a significant literature. Each of their views has strong advocates. None, however, has to this point, culminated in a groundswell of shared attention to the adaptive

---

1. In an important work on educational imagination Elliot W. Eisner has a more limited concern. He critiques the preoccupation in much educational literature and policy discussions with the control of learning sequences and the quest for predictable and measurable outcomes; *The Educational Imagination*, 17–23.

2. Publications of these contributors to the discussions on the shape of Christian religious education are included in the bibliography.

challenge of re-invigorating the religious traditions of the old mainline Protestant denominations through the faith-forming education of their children and youth.[3]

When I call for a new educational *imagination* of faith formation, I have in mind something broader than Maria Harris' important exploration of teaching as an "activity of religious imagination"[4] or Eliot Eisner's call for "deep thinking" about curriculum and the competencies needed for participation in contemporary society.[5] Instead, my attention is drawn to the *agency of the collective imagination* of congregations and their religious traditions in forming and transforming the faith of their members. My thinking, in other words, has been more influenced by the questions and insights of theologians, historians, sociologists, and anthropologists exploring the continuity and renewal of community values and practices in the midst of often radical change. This quest has occupied my personal attention for many years. Only recently, however, have I realized the extent to which my questions continued to reflect the influence of the "technical rationality" Eisner and Harris challenged. Only recently have I also realized that during the past several years I may also have witnessed several congregations whose educational imaginations had transformed their practices of faith-forming education. In their experience, I am increasingly convinced, we may discern clues for a more general and expansive discussion of a faith-forming education that if embraced, may culminate in the revitalization of the faith traditions of the old mainline Protestant denominations.

An Example of Educational Imagination in Adaptive Change

One example from the 1970s, when some congregations were first becoming aware of the adaptive challenges ahead of them, may illustrate my point.

---

3. The discussion that follows will focus on the agency of the shared life of congregations in forming the faith of children and youth. A still more challenging task confronts the congregations of the old mainline Protestant denominations; namely, to re-envision the agency of schooling or academies in forming faith. The Sunday school may today be a convenient place for children to be in church, but it no longer enjoys the reinforcing structures that once underscored its usefulness in a faith-forming education. The weekday school may strengthen the faith-forming education of some evangelical Protestants and Roman Catholics, but the commitment of most mainline Protestants to public education means they have to think creatively about other approaches to the disciplines of learning associated with schooling.

4. Harris, *Teaching and Religious Imagination*, xv.

5. Eisner, *The Educational Imagination*, 4ff.

At the time our family participated in a quite new congregation located in a rapidly growing suburb on the edge of a large midwestern city. Many young families had, like ours, been attracted to this congregation by the excellence of the preaching of the senior minister and a deep commitment among many of its members to the Sunday school for their children.

We soon discovered, however, that many of these young parents had moved to the city from small midwestern communities and congregations. They desired a creative Sunday school program for their children. They wanted something different, however, from their childhood memories of pedantic teachers and boring Sunday school classes. They appreciated preaching that challenged them, but few were interested in any kind of adult education. The pastors made several efforts to entice them into a variety of adult education experiences with little success. Then they began to think deeply about alternatives to existing traditional patterns of education in their denomination.

That spring they recruited several people to help plan the congregation's worship for the following Advent season. Over the next several months the group studied biblical texts for the Advent season with one of the pastors. They reviewed liturgies associated with the season. They considered the role of music and different forms of art appropriate to the season. They identified ways to engage children and youth with the stories, music, and symbols of the season at home and in the church. Each moment in this process drew them into critical theological reflection on the content of their decisions. It took more time than the pastor and Christian educator had anticipated. Their initial commitment to collaboration required patience while committee members explored with them primary texts and resources and became familiar with practices associated with celebrating the season. Eventually, however, the committee developed plans for each of the worship services in that liturgical season and designed strategies to prepare people of all ages in the congregation during autumn to participate more fully in the plans they were developing. Participation of all ages in the worship services of Advent and Christmas was high and enthusiastic. The experiment was considered successful. Then the congregation decided to approach the preparation of the congregation for the seasons of Lent and Easter and later, the season of Pentecost, in the same way.

I knew something significant was happening when more than fifty persons participated in each of the different seasonal learning and planning committees, and when youth were included on the planning committees, the choir commissioned new anthems, the sermons of the clergy began to include tactile examples and moments of theater, children urged their parents to sit in the front rows during worship so they could see "what was happening," a significant number of families made use of resources prepared by the committees for study and worship in their homes, a growing number of artists attracted to the congregation by its growing interest in the contribution of the arts to worship visually transformed the space in which we worshipped, and several years later when attendance for Pentecost Sunday was comparable to that on Easter. The impact became even more evident in the growing interest of congregational members in exploring increasingly difficult questions about the relationship of their faith to the social, political, and economic problems of the community in which we lived. I think I now know why.

Through this explicitly educational process, this congregation's children, youth, and adults had become caught up in the "creative appropriation" of the events of Jesus' life and ministry embedded in the liturgical seasons of Advent, Lent, Easter, and Pentecost. As they participated in these events they became increasingly open to their claims and discovered in them meanings to center their lives. Although I found the experience exhilarating at the time, I now recognize the catalyst to the transformations of faith in this congregation originated in the theologically grounded exercise of the educational imaginations of the pastors and a few lay leaders. It then expanded as members of the congregation increasingly probed their expectations for their preparation to participate in each of these liturgical seasons.

By an educational imagination capable of forming faith I have in mind Maxine Greene's description of the human capacity for assembling a "coherent world." This world lies beyond what R. Smithson once called the "illusory babels," the "odd intersections of meaning, strange corridors of history, unexpected echoes, unknown humors," as it accounts for new inventions and unexpected interventions that bring "us together in community."[6] Imagination in this sense, Greene adds, "enables us to cross not only the empty spaces between ourselves" and those whom we have often called "other," but also between ourselves and the void separating ourselves from the mystery we call "God." It gives form to the "re-assembling" that occurs in our quests of faithful and creative "remembering" in the midst of the changing circumstances of our lives. It moves us beyond the recollection of events of the past, including those in the Bible and our religious traditions,

---

6. Greene, *Teacher as Stranger*, 2–3.

to participation in them. Greene goes on to describe the imagination as the one cognitive capacity that "permits us to give credence to alternative realities. It allows us to break with the taken for granted, to set aside familiar distinctions and definitions,"[7] and to see possibility in the midst of apparent hopelessness and loss.

Craig Dykstra, quoting Mary Warnock, has called the imagination the capacity of "seeing in depth." It is "the capacity to perceive the 'more' in what is already before us." It provides the impetus "to see beneath the surface of things, to get beyond the obvious and the merely conventional, to note the many aspects of any particular situation." The imagination, in other words, enables us "to attend to the deep meanings of things"[8] that eventually lead us into a deeper knowledge of God and our relationship to the world around us. From this perspective it is the capacity that enables us to break out of our preoccupation with educational programs, missional activities, and worship services to see the creative and redemptive activity of God in a child's anticipation of a story of faithfulness we are about to tell, in the reconciling handshake of folks with deeply different values and beliefs, in the intensity of a congregation's corporate prayer; in other words, in the most common of our practices of teaching and learning, serving, caring, and worshiping. In these moments we may begin to discern that in the practices of sharing life together in a community of faith the imagination has a distinctively ecclesial shape and character.

Educational Imagination in Congregational Life

The lack of imagination can be a deadly thing. The lack of a theologically grounded educational imagination can be especially disastrous for a congregation. This is especially true for congregations struggling to respond to their changing circumstances. As I have participated in that struggle over the years, seven themes have increasingly dominated my own imagination about what the education of congregations might look like in forming and transforming the faith of children and youth within the agency of their religious traditions. A caveat must be noted here. My description of these themes is a general one. The educational imagination of specific congregations must be further developed and refined with insights from their own

7. Ibid.

8. Dykstra, "Pastoral and Ecclesial Imagination," 48.

theological traditions and practices, modes of thinking, and ways of living together faithfully in the variety of their social and cultural contexts.

1. *An education that forms the faith of children and youth builds up and equips congregations (and their religious traditions) to be the body of Christ in the world.* A faith-forming education may do many things, but if it does not engage young people in the disciplines of developing proficiency in the ecclesial practices of worshiping God and serving neighbor, it is a sham. It is a noisy gong or clanging cymbal. This primary *aim* of a congregation's faith-forming education is shared by all denominational traditions. Its focus should not be to save young people from the world but rather to prepare them to participate in the world in response to God's salvific care of the whole of creation. From this perspective, a faith-forming education seeks to incorporate young people into contemporary extensions of the ministry of Jesus. Participation in that ministry requires knowledge (in the biblical experiential sense of embodied and enacted knowing) of the creative and redemptive activity of God and of the world as the context for God's creative and redemptive work.

The implications are several. A faith-forming education in congregations involves young people in the practices and perspectives, sensibilities and habits associated with being the body of Christ in ministry in the world. It draws young people and their adult mentors into the maintenance, renewal, and transformation of their ecclesial traditions as agents of the creative activity of God in a constantly changing world. Young people, consequently, are not the focus of a congregation's education. Their preparation to participate in and celebrate Christ's ministry is.[9] This leads me to a second affirmation regarding the shape of a faith-forming education in congregations and their religious traditions.

2. *To engage children and youth in building up and equipping the church as the body of Christ in ministry in the world plunges a congregation (and the agencies of its religious tradition) necessarily into ecclesially grounded educational practices of forming and transforming faith.* This inherently communal theological task gives form to a congregation's catechetical culture, in which the gifts and graces of young people might be nurtured. St. Paul makes the point. To each of us is given some manifestation of the Spirit "for the common good."[10] The consequence is that if one of us hurts, we all

9. For an extended elaboration of this point see Mercer, *Welcoming Children*, especially chapters 5 and 6.

10. 1 Cor 12:7.

hurt; if one of us is honored, we are all honored.[11] No distinctions of age can be found here.

To "build up" and "equip" are educational categories. They convey the movement from incomplete to complete, from novitiate to expert, from unskilled to skilled, from ignorance to knowledge, from naïveté to wisdom, from injustice to justice, from lacking faith to being filled with faith, from being reconciled to reconciling. As the ecclesial embodiment of Christ's ministry in the present age, we do not arrive on the scene ready to do battle with the forces of evil and injustice or to be agents of God's hospitality and reconciling love. We enter into the forms of Christ's ministry as neophytes. We learn how to live into expectations of competency in that ministry by participating in them.

These themes run deep in the biblical record. Some are explicit. Moses instructed the Israelites to educate their children so they, their children, and their children's children would not forget to worship God in the strange, but Promised Land, lying before them. Some themes are implicit. The commandment first articulated by Moses to love God with *all* our heart, soul, and might is an example. Since our capacities develop as we age, to love with *all* our being is something we can potentially embody at any age and yet, must also continuously *grow* into as we age. It requires the continuity of practicing that love as we grow from childhood into adolescence and then into adulthood through the constantly changing circumstances in the always changing situations of our lives.

The same point is made frequently in the hymnody of the church. The "Spirit of God," as one hymn declares,[12] may fall constantly "afresh on us." We take on that spirit, however, only as it "melts" our self-serving ways, "molds" us into the shape of the cross, "fills" us with the freedom to love unconditionally, and tests us as we are used in God's ministries of love and reconciliation. This takes time. Indeed, it takes up all the time. And it takes a community of nurture and the reinforcing influence of its religious tradition to lead, support, and sustain us through that lifelong effort.

Dorothy Bass and Craig Dykstra highlight the process I am describing in their discussion of Christian practices. They define Christian practices as the things "Christian people do together over time in response to and in the light of God's active presence for the life of the world."[13] Christian practices,

11. 1 Cor 12:26.

12. Iverson, "Spirit of the Living God," *United Methodist Hymnal*, 393.

13. Dykstra and Bass, "Times of Yearning," 5.

they emphasize, "address fundamental human needs and conditions through concrete human acts." Feeding, healing, reconciling, praying, caring for others would be examples. These are occasions for encountering the mystery of God in the midst of the mystery of living. Practices are something "done together" by members of all ages in Christian communities "over time." They are repeated often enough across the life span so that they seem the natural thing to do. Christian practices "possess standards of excellence." They are measured, in other words, against the extent to which they reveal the creative and redemptive activity of God at work in the world. Since we are finite, this standard encourages our quest to grow in faith and wisdom throughout our lives. The educative potential in the repetition of the practices of Christian community occurs in the always new discovery that our "daily lives are all tangled up with the things God is doing in the world."[14]

The biblical witness provides many clues to these practices of Christian community. Bass and Dykstra describe several, including hospitality, household economics, and keeping the Sabbath. Two sets of practices, however, establish the context for all others. The first centers on loving God with all our heart, mind, soul, and strength. From this perspective it is not enough for a congregation to nurture the religious experience or increase the body of religious knowledge of young people. A ministry of faith-forming education directed wholly to loving God involves the development of moral, spiritual, mental, and bodily habits, sensibilities, perspectives, and skills for the giving of ourselves fully in response to God's love for all creation.

The second commandment follows, involving us in practices of learning to love the neighbors we meet in God's creation as we love ourselves. Again the standards for living into this commandment are clarified by the Gospel writers. The Gospel of Matthew, for example, spells out one set of implications of this commandment in the twenty-fifth chapter in descriptions of feeding the hungry, comforting the sick, and visiting the imprisoned. We do not do these things naturally. They must be learned in a community that feeds the hungry, comforts the sick, and visits the imprisoned.

3. *A faith-forming education requires the interdependence of the generations.* The word *youth* has no meaning without notions of *childhood* and *adulthood*. In similar fashion notions of child and adult are inextricably linked to our views of youth. Our use of each of these terms, however, tends to be slippery. Educational theorist and social critic Henry Giroux makes the point in his observation that the notion of youth or adolescence

14. Ibid., 7–8.

functions as a "complex, shifting, and contradictory category" through which the American U.S. public "registers its own crisis of meaning, vision, and community."[15] He could be referring to the range of definitions of youth found in the writings of psychologists or to the images of youth reflected in the media. Both are prevalent in the marketing of youth ministry resources and programs. His observation, however, grows out of an awareness of the contradiction in our fascination with the idea of youth evident in advertising images of young people and our marginalization of young people in the policy and power conversations of our institutions.

Giroux is not the first to note ambiguity in American cultural views of young people. As far back as the 1960s sociologist Paul Goodman explored the absurdity of their place and experience in much of American life. More recently youth advocate Mike Males has called our attention to the cultural function of youth scapegoats. Even more recently, religious educator Katherine Turpin has explored the influence of consumer culture in shaping the faith of youth.

Considerations of the intergenerational interdependence of a faith-forming education might begin with the emphasis given in the biblical witness to the mutuality of youthful vision and elderly wisdom. There we discover notions of wisdom and vision both originate in a consciousness of the presence of God, a sense of participation in the mystery of God's creative and redeeming work. With a short view of the past, the vision of young people is deepened and tested against the wisdom of their elders. The wisdom of the aged, whose experience of the past is long and whose anticipation of the future is short, is refined by the sense of possibility among children and youth. The continuing vitality of a community depends on their mutuality. This suggests that in forming and transforming the faith of young people, teenagers need to mentor at least one child in the life of faith over a long enough period of time to see the results of their efforts. At the same time, children need to have at some point teenage mentors to support their journey through developmental challenges they will soon face. Every young person needs to be mentored by elders across the span of young, middle, and older adulthood. Every child needs to have the experience of showing some teenager and some adult a new way of perceiving, thinking, or doing something that has meaning for both of them. And just as important, every teenager needs to mentor at least one adult into perspectives

15. Giroux, "Teenage Sexuality, Body Politics, and the Pedagogy of Display," 24.

and sensibilities located in the distinctive theological negotiations of adolescents with the issues and circumstances of their lives.

These are typically long-term relationships. Two or three conversations with a chosen adult mentor during confirmation may be helpful, but they are not adequate in a ministry of formation and transformation. Without some sustained pattern of intergenerational learning the formative faith experiences of young people are more likely to alienate them from the communities of faith with which they could identify, leave them without memories of hope to enliven their future, and diminish their sense of responsibility for the well-being of the community and the earth that is both their home and the well spring of their vocations in the world.

4. *The responsibility of mentoring the faith of children and youth belongs to the whole congregation in the full range of its ministries.* This view of mentoring challenges the tendency in congregations to limit their view of education to the school of the congregation and its designated teachers and administrators. It involves much more. Religious educator Gabriel Moran helpfully points out that if we take the root meanings of "to teach" as "to show" or "show how" seriously, this should be obvious.[16] His insight has several implications. It expands our view of who teaches from those designated for the role in a classroom to anyone with enough expertise to introduce another person into the more complex knowing and doing required for participating in some task or event. It redirects the attention of those who teach from being concerned about the extent to which learners "know how" to their proficiency in "learning how."[17] It privileges pedagogical expertise in modeling, advising, and guiding we typically associate with practices of mentoring rather than the telling and presenting we more often identify with practices of classroom instruction. Perhaps most important it highlights the community as mentor/teacher in which no one, yet everyone, may move in and out of the interplay of teaching and learning, of forming and being formed.

The most effective way to learn to speak English, for example, is to grow up in an English-speaking community. The clearest way of learning to be Christian or Hindu, Methodist or Catholic, is to participate with others in the practices of being Christian or Hindu, Methodist or Catholic. In this sense we may all potentially mentor someone at the threshold of expertise in some shared community practice. I am reminded of children who have

16. Moran, *Showing How*, 37.

17. Ibid., 38.

shown me how to participate in the praying practice of their families or some informal church gathering. I think of teenagers who showed the members of a congregation we once attended how to serve a meal in a homeless shelter or to conduct Bible study with the homebound members of their congregation. And I am reminded of wise elders who modeled for children, youth, and adults around them possibilities of faithfulness at the end of life. Any worship service, congregational dinner, mission trip, or committee meeting, in other words, becomes an opportunity for "mentoring" faith among those learning how to participate in it. As their participants show each other how to participate in the event, to make sense of some idea or thought introduced or discussed during the event, or to reflect on what their participation might mean or require, the locus of the teaching and learning almost floats around the room. In moments like these a child may well become mentor to an adult. A youth may lead a child. An adult may establish more rigorous expectations for the competent participation of everyone. The patterns of teaching and learning in forming faith to be found in their relationships with each other become even more explicit in a fifth feature in a congregation's educational imagination.

5. *As congregations engage in practices of mentoring to build up and equip the church as the body of Christ in ministry in the world, the diversity of the gifts and graces of young people is nurtured.* Despite the common historical context the children and youth in any generation share, they still make sense of and respond to their engagement with the gospel and the world in diverse ways. This insight, however, has not tended to inform approaches to Christian education or youth ministry for most of its contemporary history.

For decades Christian educators and youth ministry advocates tried, instead, to fit all young people into some normative appropriation of the developmental categories of Havighurst, Erikson, Piaget, Kohlberg, and Fowler. Then we became aware of the influence of social, cultural, and economic contexts on young people so, in recent years, we have made distinctions among young people on the basis of generational markers distinguishing for example, generation "x" from generation "y" from the millennial generation. For most of its history the education for faith of children and youth in the churches of old mainline Protestant and Catholic denominations has been shaped by white and middle class values, perspectives, and concerns. As such it failed to convey gospel for vast numbers of youth who were not white, middle class, or mainline. Amazingly absent from most youth ministry literature until recently were insights from the faith journeys of youth in congregations reflecting African, Asian, Hispanic, or Native American cultural traditions. As amazing is the silence over the impact of the "savage inequalities" Jonathan Kozol[18] and others have described among the young in our schools, or of the "cold new world" William Finnegan observed among teenagers lacking the support of the mediating institutions of family, church, school, law, or social services.[19] Little attention has generally been given in our congregations to the deep theological and ethical questions young people are asking. As invisible in our congregations are gay and lesbian youth and young people with handicapping conditions.

My image of a faith-forming education was enlarged significantly several years ago during a Pentecost Sunday worship service in the congregation we attended. The liturgy had been developed over a period of several months by youth and adults from the several different nations that made up this congregation. The youth, ranging in age from thirteen through twenty, took on the task of recreating and dramatizing the Pentecost story for the sermon. It required mentoring from the pastoral staff, youth leaders, and parents. It required repetitive rehearsals to ensure the worthiness of their effort. Through this liturgical moment they shared individual and collective gifts of writing and speaking, theological reflection and biblical interpretation, dancing, singing, and praying. The climax of the drama occurred when the young people (black, white, and brown, male and female, middle and low income, all from a variety of family structures and several different nations) kneeled around the communion table to lead the congregation in the Lord's Prayer in their own languages. In Spanish, Italian, Mano, and other tribal languages of West Africa and in the dialects of English from the Deep South, Barbados, Jamaica, and Liberia they revealed that the praise of God does, in fact, require all the languages of humanity as well as a variety of prayer forms. The diversity, rather than the homogeneity of their gifts, became the catalyst to their shared experience in the church as the body of Christ. This is the same group of youth mentioned earlier who met for Bible study in the homes of shut-ins, who initiated and led the congregation in a ministry of feeding the homeless, and who participated self-consciously in judicatory youth meetings to subvert the racism and social class bias they encountered there. This approach to youth ministry did not occur by happenstance. This diverse group of young people had been mentored by adults who envisioned a different kind of church and world through the mentoring they had received from their attention to the youth in their midst.

18. Kozol, *Savage Inequalities*.

19. Finnegan, *Cold New World*.

6. *A faith-forming education must be contextually relevant.* In the 1960s we assumed the world was divided between the sacred and secular and that secularization was the greatest challenge to a congregation's efforts to form the faith of their children and youth. That division, if it still exists in the public consciousness, has changed radically. Dimensions of the religious permeate popular culture. The religious environment in and through which young people move today is more like that of Corinth and Athens than that of our perceptions of the 1950s. Old and new religious movements co-exist. The human quest for the transcendent and for meaning is nurtured in popular concerts, through the media of film and gaming, through practices of self discipline, through efforts to protect the environment, and by gurus who market the practices of their own religious experience. Religious perspectives once considered heretical by an ancient church have found new and unquestioning adherents. Religious syncretism creeps into the practices of the most traditional of religious communities. Movies and computerized games convey images of the sacred and the demonic with little distinction. New media technologies and the Internet provide a plethora of options for religious inquiry.

In the midst of this situation, interpreters of the contemporary religious scene claim that the quest for spirituality, especially among the young, has taken precedence over the historic quest to identify with a religious tradition. The context for the church's faith-forming educational efforts, in other words, looks more like a shopping mall of religious options begging for the attention of young consumers of religious experience. So we are no longer surprised to find teenagers with tattoos wearing tee-shirts with religious symbols blazoned across their chests who regularly read the Bible, refuse to eat meat out of respect for the lives of animals, resist participation in congregational worship, wouldn't miss the latest vampire movie, experiment with Zen meditation practices, attend Christian rock concerts, assume that after death they will return reincarnated in some other life form, or deny evolutionary theory while envisioning careers dependent on that same theory. Even teenagers who seem to reflect more traditional responses to the gospel assume that the authority for their faith decisions is located in their personal preferences rather than in the interplay of the work of the Holy Spirit and the religious tradition which informs their faith. The dynamics of the pluralism in what Wade Clark Roof has called the "spiritual marketplace," in other words, tests the credibility of the message and practices of most congregational efforts at forming the faith of their young people.

Another significant contextual challenge may be traced to the very different experience of the meaning of time and space among contemporary youth. My original insight into this possibility came through Margaret Mead's little book *Culture and Commitment*, which I read many years ago. She argued at the time, that only those born after World War II were natives of the contemporary world.[20] I have since realized the same could be said for those born after Sputnik in 1957, again for those born after the proliferation of computer technologies, and now for those born into an era of cloning life forms and gene pool mapping. Consequences embedded in each innovation not only alter the world views held by preceding generations, they require new theological articulations to make sense of inherited beliefs and practices.

To make her argument for difference in the education of the only natives of the late twentieth century, Mead identifies three social processes of community formation.[21] In the first, people educated their children so as to perpetuate their assumptions and practices through them into the future. Paolo Freire calls this a banking view of education. This view, I would suggest, continues to dominate most discussions in our churches on the transmission of doctrine. It is the primary pedagogical approach to faith formation in faith communities dominated by charismatic personalities or formulas of belief and morality. The focus of attention is on the imitation and replication of that which is received through some educational activity. Little attention is given, consequently, to the originality of the voices or the faithfulness of young people or to the disruption of inherited practices and beliefs by changing social conditions or new scientific or technological knowledge.

In the second social process identified by Mead, communities educate their children with the expectation they would have to adapt what they learned for situations and circumstances unknown to their parents and mentors.[22] John Dewey's discovery-oriented view of education, for example, provided a way for community leaders to prepare young people to solve problems they had not themselves encountered and to develop answers to questions they had not yet asked. This view dominated my own approach to the educational ministries of the congregations I served in the 1960s. It continues to influence the assumptions about faith formation in most old

20. Mead, *Culture and Commitment*, 70–71.
21. Ibid., 13ff.
22. Ibid., 39ff.

mainline Protestant denominations and their congregations. The emphasis is on exploration and the discovery of personal meaning, all too often with little grounding in the heritage of their communities.

In her third category, Mead suggests we need to consider processes of formation and education that include all ages as teachers and learners.[23] Hierarchical and historical patterns of authority, consequently, are turned upside down. Nowhere is this more evident than in a comparison of the competencies of children and their parents in the virtual worlds of computerized technology. The insight, however, is not new. Jesus set a child in the midst of the disciples as an example for their own faithfulness. In the virtual world that engages our computer literate young people, however, the view of time and space that has influenced most views of education in the past no longer holds their attention. Time does not flow from past to present to future. All three dimensions of time are fully contained in episodes of digitalized time and in the penetrable boundaries of virtual time.

Spatial boundaries linking cultural identity and experience with geographical locations have similarly been transgressed. If they have the resources, contemporary young people move through the diverse cultural terrain of the globe with amazing confidence. If not, they have still been nurtured by a media world of momentarily intensified and generally blurred boundaries. Plurality, change, and relativity are the constants in their experience, not the homogeneity, tradition, and constancy our ancestors assumed. In our quest to be relevant to the differences in their experience, we have tried to pin down the characteristics of each generation to develop ministries that account for that experience. Those of us who are not native to these emerging worldviews inevitably cannot fully understand either their assumptions or the ways they structure their experience. We are outsiders.

This discovery is not something to frighten or discourage us. Rather it should deepen our engagement with the resources of our religious traditions in the quest for educational patterns of faith formation responsive to the contextual realities of contemporary young people. That educational insight is at the heart of the deuteronomic instructions for educating the next generation. The questions of children, those who knew nothing but the challenges of living in the Promised Land, prompt the stories of their elders' experience of God in the wilderness. Children hear the stories of their elders, however, through their experience of living in the cities and on the farms of that Promised Land. In their hearing they discover resources

23. Ibid., 65ff.

in those ancient stories unavailable to the imaginations of their elders. As they make sense of what they have heard in their different context, they become teachers to their teachers' teaching.

In the previous chapter I argued that a more useful metaphor for thinking about the processes of a faith forming education may be located in the celebration of the originating and intensifying events of a community. They are the participatory symbols of God's activity. They form the curricular infrastructure of congregational life, including, but not limited to Advent, Christmas, Epiphany, Lent, Mothers Day, Homecoming, the fall revival, and mission trips. They are contexts for encountering and nurturing our sensibilities to the presence of the holy. They create space for the intensification of our experience of community that anthropologist Victor Turner and much later, James Carse, called *communitas*. An event has a past, a present, and a future. Indeed, an event transposes the relationship of past, present, and future. They do not flow sequentially from one to the other. They are embedded in each other and yet, they also create trajectories of experience through time and in space.

Note this pattern in the church's witness to the resurrection in the Eucharistic liturgy. Ten simple words, beginning with: "Christ has died." Something happened in the past. In our encounter with that truth it happens again. Christ dies and in our faithlessness, Christ will die again. "Christ is risen." This affirmation is real in the experience of Mary and the disciples, but a new possibility for any person on some contemporary road to Emmaus. The Christ who came, and is here, moreover, will also "come again." In this juxtaposition of time past, present, and future this primary event in the faith of Christians becomes revelatory in the specificity of our contexts. It not only illuminates the course of our lives; it gives form and thereby meaning to them.

In events time functions polyphonically. The rhythms of past, present, and future co-exist. This may be an awkward concept to grasp for many folk my age, but it is not confusing for many of today's young people. They move with amazing ease in and out of the rhythms of rock and Bach and rap and reggae and back to plainsong. Despite our adult tendencies to pigeonhole the cultural expressions of young people in the songs they sing, they move easily through the cadences of the spirituals, rock, folk, and Genevan psalter, *if,* that is, they are familiar with these various musical forms. This mobility is deeply rooted in their experience. Many of us watch with amazement as young people appear simultaneously to watch television, work the Internet, and complete a homework assignment. We should not be amazed, however, for time functions multi-dimensionally for them.

So does their experience of space or place. Images function in holographic more than representational ways. The here and there of space are transposed against each other in the now and then. This means, for example, that in an era of space exploration the up of heaven and down of hell are meaningless designations. Theological categories framed in a Ptolemaic cosmology only make sense when transformed by insights from Einsteinian relativity. We hold these worldviews in tension with every recitation of the Apostles' Creed. Familiar images such as Leonardo da Vinci's vision of the Last Supper move off the wall and into our lives through pictures of homeless folk eating with the members of a congregation in some church basement.

It is from this perspective that I developed an increasing appreciation for the multidimensional and multifaceted life of faith in the congregation where the members ate in "each other's homes all the time" described in the last chapter. Memories of breaking bread in biblical, historical, and contemporary settings intruded upon and transformed their own practices of eating and talking together. In this congregation two or three children or youth might show up for Sunday school. The youth "group" gathered only as the Spirit moved someone in the congregation to call them together. But the children and youth of this congregation were deeply involved in its worship life and outreach ministries. They were amazingly conversant with the stories and teachings of the Bible. They showed up for meetings when the topics of discussions interested them. They participated in congregational work parties. Why? I would suggest it had to do, in part, with their experience of being welcomed into the fellowship of eating and talking together around the tables of that congregation in homes, fellowship hall, and sanctuary. In the repetition of practices associated with this Eucharistic event, they experienced themselves in an upper room sharing the Passover feast with disciples of all ages through the ages. They listened in on and often contributed to conversations among adults to make sense of these events in their lives. They heard as well, stories of the pain of meals prepared and served to white folk by black folk and of black folk eating the leftovers in back rooms. They celebrated the shattering of that latter set of memories in the context of the promise of new life every time they together broke the bread of reconciliation at the communion rail, during some covered dish supper, or in each others' homes.

New technologies further contribute to the polyphonic and holographic capacity of today's children and youth to envision their participation in God's creative and redemptive activity in new ways. Tom Beaudoin has argued forcefully for the creative potential for faithfulness in the ambiguity, irreverence, and suffering that distinguishes the faith of young people formed by the worldviews of the new technologies.[24] The illusions of virtual reality, however, are not the same thing as the mystery of God beyond both our experience of the real world and our illusions of the virtual world. Again the image of the holograph becomes helpful. The images of faith for contemporary young people are not only drawn from the transposition of past, present, and future, but also from the resources of the imagination as it engages them. It is difficult to critique imaginative illusions in linear patterns of thinking without dismissing them. In the holograph, however, each of these sources of images for forming faith fill the imagination, modify and test each other, because each is subject to the mystery in God that is the context for all our responses of faith. As we engage that multifaceted context, we are challenged to be bold and to think imaginatively about the participation of young people in an education directed to the formation and transformation of their faith. That challenge suggests a way of thinking about pedagogical practices that influence the purposes and shape of education in forming faith in congregations and through those congregations in their religious traditions. This challenge transforms their quests into possibilities for the future through their children and youth.

7. *A faith-forming education relevant to the challenges of our contemporary experience engages congregations in the preparation of their children, youth, and adults to participate in the events central to their identity as Christian communities.* The pedagogical practices involved in this affirmation are familiar to anyone who has planned something as intimate as a birthday party or as public as a congregationally-based community mission project. They are focused on the celebration of the events that give rise to, nurture, reinforce, and sustain our faith as individuals and congregations and in the outpouring of our concern for the well-being of creation that some have identified with the "common good." Many of these events occur in most, if not all congregations. Some are locally specific. Others gather folks into celebrations transcending and incorporating local communities into the traditions of a denomination or the larger Christian and inter-faith communities. In each instance, they have the potential to be catalysts to

24. Beaudoin, *Virtual Faith.*

expanding conversations among those involved about how these events shape and form lives of faith. These theologically grounded pedagogical practices include in some form at least the following.

- *The practice of anticipation.* The practice of anticipation depends on the vitality of our memories of the presence and activity of God. It is intensified in and sustained through congregational conversations. As we approach an event memories from past events fill its possibilities with significance and meaning. They are something we have to talk about. We need time to talk about them in some depth. The practice of anticipation, consequently, involves the repetition of stories from the past associated with the event we are anticipating. The medium of our storytelling may include a variety of forms. Narratives may be the most common. Songs have also been important sources for this remembering. Symbols and artifacts typically evoke memories of possibility. The act of memory, however, is also an act of assessment, of critical reflection on the extent to which the community has been faithful to the intent of the original event and the potential in the event to empower some new future for the community. So practices of anticipation originate in and are sustained by the interplay of our memories and our critiques of our attempts to embody and give form to them.

- *The practice of preparation.* In this practice we make decisions about needed resources and their usefulness for our participation in the anticipated event. We immerse ourselves in Sunday school classes, worship services, family night suppers, retreats, and after school programs in the heritage of our religious tradition to discover connections between our past, present, and future. We script our participation in the event. The expansiveness and candor of that script is a test of a congregation's hospitality. It establishes the course of our engagement with the event, its meanings, and expectations. It becomes the curriculum guiding our engagement with the possibilities of the event. As we consider our participation in the event we clarify its meaning and significance for us. We put it into historical, social, and theological perspective. We make plans for the setting in which we will participate in the event. This may be one of the most important elements in a ministry of formation and education among children and youth. As with the preparation involved in the celebration of any major event, it takes time, indeed, much more time than many congregations currently give to them. When I wonder why the Eucharist may well be the deepest well spring for my own faith journey, I am drawn back to summer church camp in which the closing communion service was the liturgical as well as programmatic high point of the week. All through the week we made preparations similar to those of a hostess preparing for a dinner party. We read and re-read the liturgical text to the point we could almost recite it from memory. We tested our ideas against denominational teachings and traditions in formal small group discussions with camp counselors. We rehearsed the hymns and responses until we could sing some of them from memory. We chose and prepared a site for our gathering. Our preparation of that site reflected the themes of our general discussion during the week. Our mentors asked questions to help us think through the extent to which we were responsible to meanings located in that first Last Supper and to the traditions of our denomination extending those meanings into the present age. In these practices of preparation we were not only developing the knowledge and skill for confident participation in this event, we were laying the groundwork for future encounters with its claim on our lives.

- *The practice of rehearsal.* Liturgy and mission are both gifts we offer in response to the graciousness of God. The criteria for our responsiveness is found in the gift of the widow, in the sharing of church members of all they had with each other, and in the candor of a child's question. This does not just happen. It involves rehearsal. Which hymns do we most love? The ones we most often sing! Why? Because the words and rhythms are not strange, but deeply engrained in our minds and bodies. Through the practice of rehearsing these songs we develop the expertise for learning how to sing others. The same is true of any act of ministry. Ministries of compassion, forgiveness, or service are awkward until they have been practiced to the point of habituated expertise. The practice of rehearsal often begins in what a colleague once called "a sheltered try" or safe enactment of whatever competency is expected for one's participation in an event. Through practices of rehearsal young people develop the confidence and skill to speak themselves into places of power in congregations and communities. They develop the strength of character to offer prayers on behalf of their peers and of the whole congregation. They develop the skill to share their knowledge of their faith heritage in some form of public witness. They develop habit memories that give form to their deepening convictions in acts of serving others. In the midst of our rehearsal our anticipation is intensified, our competencies refined, and our capacities for critical reflection expanded.

- *The practice of participation.* We do it. We worship. We study. We pray. We confront a political figure with questions about his or her views on the environment. We ask questions that push the boundaries of our knowledge and experience. We become friends to an elderly person in poor health without family. We comfort the sick, visit the imprisoned, feed the hungry. We play in ways that build up rather than hurt others. We strategize some missional project. We speak from the traditions of justice in our religious tradition to some disparity in the economic, political, or educational life of our communities. Participation in this sense is empowered responsiveness. In the practice of participation we discover the spontaneity associated with competence and expertise. In our participation we witness to the significance of the event in our response to the activity of God in our lives.

- *The practice of critical reflection.* In this practice we look back on our experience of any part of an event, test it against the corporate memory of our community of faith, examine it for possibilities for faith we had not previously anticipated, and construct a story for future remembering. In this step we shape and intensify our memory of our experience of the event. We clarify its relationship to the events that preceded and influenced it. We make decisions about our relation to their deepest meanings and demands on our lives. In this process we are drawn into the interplay of celebration in which we experience the exhilaration of authenticity in our living into the event and confession through which we acknowledge the finitude of our attempts to embody the significance of that event for the church and world. Through this practice children and youth develop capacities for shaping the future of their engagement with the gospel.

These pedagogical practices in a faith-forming education appear to occur sequentially, but that is not the case in most of our experience. Often the process begins with participation, which creates the conditions for anticipation, which may lead us into the disciplined practices of preparation. Sometimes we begin with preparation that creates anticipation for engagement. Other times we begin with questions for critical reflection that set the stage for the preparation that creates in us a sense of anticipation and leads us, subsequently, into the rehearsal of our engagement with some event central to our faith tradition.

Concluding Reflections

Just a decade ago we crossed another major marker in the passage of time. Those of us following the Gregorian calendar entered a new millennium. As we crossed this threshold in time, those of us in congregations associated with the old mainline Protestant denominations were confronted with a decision similar to one facing the ancestors of our faith on the banks of the Jordan River, in Babylon, in ancient Roman cities, and on the edges of the American frontier. In each of these confrontations with changes of social or temporal location, community elders committed themselves to the education of the community to ensure the continuity of their witness to the creative and redemptive activity of God in their new settings through their children. It is not clear to me, however, that the elders of our congregations or in our denominational agencies share the sense of the urgency evident in the imaginative proposals of Moses for living in the Promised Land, of the Apostle Paul in building up and equipping new congregations around the Mediterranean, or even of our ancestors establishing Sunday schools and congregations to counter the potential for "barbarism" on the American frontier. We seem much more interested in institutional survival or growth than in the transmission of the transformative power of our faith traditions through the generations.

I took up this project lamenting my sense of this lack of urgency among leaders in congregations and denominational agencies for the future of the church's faith. I approach its conclusion with a much keener sense of hope. Through the course of my research and writing I recalled and also observed congregations scattered here and there across the country. Like those small congregations around the Mediterranean in the first and second centuries, they have not despaired of the future in front of them. Instead they embraced a future for themselves by imaginatively involving their children and youth in the vitality of their witness to the creative and sustaining power of the Holy Spirit. Most of these congregations continued to organize classes for learners of all ages, but without the reinforcing cultural supports for their efforts they no longer relied on the efficacy of schooling to cultivate the faith of their children and youth. Rather they focused their energies on preparing their children in a variety of places to participate competently in their worship and mission: to be bearers of the gospel they proclaimed. At some point in the future, in some renewed vision of the processes of forming faith, they may reclaim a more central place for the cultivation of formally designated and trained teachers and leaders, the development of a theologically and developmentally coherent curriculum, the re-establishment of theologically grounded educational standards for professional leaders, and the reinforcement of learning faith from birth to death associated with the formal structures of catechism and schooling. That will not happen, however, until a groundswell of interest in the significance of their influence in forming faith once again catches the collective imaginations of congregational and denominational leaders.

In a sense the congregations of the old Protestant mainline denominations are living between times of vital faith-forming education in the past and new forms and approaches of education in forming the faith of young people in the future. These times of transition take time, sometimes a long time, for new patterns of formation to take root in, develop, and transform the institutional structures that prepare young people for lively worship and vital mission. The dominance of contemporary values of consumption and the pervasive influence of market strategies in our congregations at this moment in our history intensify the difficulty of this challenge. The task before us requires thoughtful and theologically grounded educational innovation on the one hand, and the patience to wait and see what comes from our efforts on the other. The most profound adaptive challenge before mainline Protestant congregations, in other words, just may be to keep focused on the responsibility of imagining a Christian religious education adequate to the task of forming the faith of our children and youth so now they, in turn, might extend their embrace of God's love for all creation to their own children.

Discussion Questions and Exercises for Personal and Group Reflection

1. How would you describe the function of educational imagination in a congregation's quest to form the faith of its children and youth? What makes the engagement of an educational imagination an ecclesial practice?

2. Which, if any, of the themes suggested in this chapter present the congregation you know best with a technical or an adaptive challenge to their practices of educating their children or youth?

3. Summarize insights from the reading of the book. At what points do they challenge your own assumptions about education in forming the faith of children and youth? And your participation or leadership in the congregation? To what extent are these technical or adaptive challenges?

4. Identify questions you have asked while reading this book that have not yet been addressed. What sources in the bibliography might help you pursue them?

5. Observe a group of children or youth in some faith-forming educational activity. Identify the range of cultural, economic, educational, family experiences, and personal interests and abilities they bring to this faith learning event. In what ways do the differences among them challenge traditional educational practices?

6. Choose an upcoming event, preferably one six to nine months away. Follow the strategic suggestions in this chapter to prepare young people to participate in it. At each step reflect on changes this process requires in the way you think about their faith formation or the way you help youth in that process. Assess whether these changes involve you in making technical or adaptive decisions. After the event is over determine what next steps need to be taken to deepen or extend the engagement of young people with its deepest meanings and claims on their lives.

Bibliography

Argyris, Chris and Schön, Donald. *Theory in Practice: Increasing Professional Effectiveness.* San Francisco: Jossey-Bass, 1974.

Bailyn, Bernard. *Education in the Forming of American Society: Needs and Opportunities for Study.* New York: Vintage Books, 1960.

Baker, Dori Grinenko. *Greenhouses of Hope: Congregations Growing Young Leaders Who Will Change the World.* Washington, DC: Alban, 2010.

Bass, Diana Butler. *Christianity after Religion: The End of the Church and the Birth of a New Spiritual Awakening.* New York: HarperOne, 2012.

———. *Christianity for the Rest of Us: How the Neighborhood Church is Transforming the Faith.* New York: HarperOne, 2006.

Bass, Dorothy C. and Craig Dykstra, eds. *For Life Abundant: Practical Theology, Theological Education, and Christian Ministry.* Grand Rapids: Eerdmans, 2008.

Bass, Dorothy C., ed. *Practicing Our Faith.* 2nd Edition. San Francisco: Jossey-Bass, 2010.

Beaudoin, Thomas. *Virtual Faith: The Irreverent Spiritual Quest of Generation X.* San Francisco: Jossey-Bass, 1998.

Bellah, Robert N. et al. *Habits of the Heart: Individualism and Commitment in American Life.* Berkeley: University of California Press, 1985.

Benner, Patricia et al. *Educating Nurses: A Call for Radical Transformation.* San Francisco: Jossey-Bass, 2010.

Berger, Peter. *The Noise of Solemn Assemblies: Christian Commitment and the Religious Establishment in America.* Garden City, NY: Doubleday, 1961.

Berryman, Jerome W. *Godly Play: An Imaginative Approach to Religious Education.* San Francisco: HarperSanFrancisco, 1991.

Bonhoeffer, Dietrich. *Life Together: A Discussion of Christian Fellowship,* translated by John W. Doberstein. New York: Harper and Row, 1954.

The Book of Discipline of the United Methodist Church 1968. Nashville: The Methodist Publishing House, 1968.

Borgmann, Albert. "On the Blessings of Calamity and the Burdens of Good Fortune," *Hedgehog Review,* Fall, 2002, 7–24.

———. *Power Failure: Christianity in the Culture of Technology.* Grand Rapids: Brazos, 2003.

Brown, Robert MacAfee. *Is Faith Obsolete?* Philadelphia: Westminster, 1974.

Browning, Robert L. "Personal Reflections: About the History of Methodist Christian Education in the Twentieth Century." Unpub., n.d.

Brueggemann, Walter. *The Creative Word: Canon as a Model for Biblical Education.* Philadelphia: Fortress, 1982.

———. "The Legitimacy of a Sectarian Hermeneutic: 2 Kings 18–19." In *Education for Citizenship and Discipleship,* edited by Mary C. Boys, 3–34. New York: Pilgrim, 1989.

Bushnell, Horace. *Christian Nurture,* edited by Luther A. Weigle. New Haven: Yale University Press, 1916; reprint 1960.

Camus, Albert. *The Plague,* translated by Stuart Gilbert. New York: Alfred A. Knopf, 1957.

Carse, James P. *The Religious Case Against Belief.* New York: Penguin, 2008.

Carter, Stephen. *Civility: Manners, Morals, and the Etiquette of Democracy.* New York: Harper Perennial, 1998.

Chopp, Rebecca. *The Power to Speak: Feminism, Language, God.* New York: Crossroad, 1991.

Cimino, Richard, and Don Lattin. *Shopping for Faith: American Religion in the New Millennium.* San Francisco: Jossey-Bass, 1998.

Cone, James H. *A Black Theology of Liberation.* Maryknoll, NY: Orbis, 1970.

Connerton, Paul. *How Societies Remember.* Cambridge: Cambridge University Press, 1989.

Cooperative Curriculum Project. *The Church's Educational Ministry: A Curriculum Plan.* St. Louis: Bethany, 1965.

Cremin, Lawrence A. *American Education: The Colonial Experience 1607–1783.* New York: Harper Torchbooks, 1970.

———. *The Genius of American Education.* New York: Vintage, 1965.

Dean, Kenda Creasy. *Practicing Passion: Youth and the Quest for a Passionate Church.* Grand Rapids: Eerdmans, 2006.

———. *What the Faith of Our Teenagers Is Telling the American Church.* New York: Oxford University Press, 2010.

Denby, David. "Influencing People: David Fincher and the 'The Social Network.'" *The New Yorker,* October 4, 2010, 98–102.

Dewey, John. *Experience and Education.* New York: Collier Books, 1938.

———. *How We Think: A Restatement of the Relation of Reflective Thinking to the Educative Process.* Boston: D. C. Heath, 1933.

Dykstra, Craig. *Growing in the Life of Faith: Education and Christian Practices.* Louisville: Geneva, 1999.

———. "Pastoral and Ecclesial Imagination." In *For Life Abundant: Practical Theology, Theological Education, and Christian Ministry,* edited by Dorothy C. Bass and Craig Dykstra, 41–61. Grand Rapids: Eerdmans, 2008.

Dykstra, Craig and Dorothy C. Bass. "Times of Yearning, Practices of Faith." *Practicing Our Faith,* edited by Dorothy C. Bass. Second edition, 41–61. San Francisco: Jossey-Bass, 2010.

Edie, Fred P. *Book Bath, Table, and Time: Christian Worship as Source and Resource for Youth Ministry.* St. Louis: Chalice, 2007.

Eisner, Elliot W. *The Educational Imagination: On the Design and Evaluation of School Programs.* New York: MacMillan, 1985.

Elkind, David. *The Hurried Child: Growing Up Too Fast Too Soon.* Reading, MA: Addison-Wesley, 1981.

Erikson, Erik H. *Childhood and Society.* New York: Norton and Norton, 1950.

Finnegan, William. *Cold New World: Growing Up in a Harder Country.* New York: Random House, 1998.

Foster, Charles R. "Curriculum and the Struggle for Power in the Church." In *Confrontation Curriculum,* edited by R. Harold Hipps, 43–64. Nashville: Christian Educators Fellowship, The United Methodist Church, 1982.

———. *Educating Congregations: The Future of Christian Education,* Second edition. Nashville: Abingdon, 2006.

———. "Proclaiming the Word with Children." In *Worship Alive.* Nashville: Discipleship Resources, n.d.

———. "Why Don't They Remember? Reflections on the Future of Congregational Education," In *Forging a Better Religious Education in the Third Millennium,* edited by James Michael Lee, 89–112. Birmingham: Religious Education, 2000.

Foster, Charles R. and Theodore Brelsford. *We Are the Church Together: Cultural Diversity in Congregational Life.* Valley Forge, PA: Trinity, 2006.

Foster, Charles R. et al. *Educating Clergy: Teaching Practices and Pastoral Imagination.* San Francisco: Jossey-Bass, 2005.

Foster, Charles R. and Fred Smith. *Black Religious Experience: Conversations on Double Consciousness and the Work of Grant Shockley.* Nashville: Abingdon, 2003.

Fowler, James W. *Stages of Faith: The Psychology of Human Development and the Quest for Meaning.* San Francisco: Harper and Row, 1981.

Freire, Paulo. *Pedagogy of the Oppressed.* New York: Continuum, 1986.

Friedenberger, Edgar. *The Vanishing Adolescent.* Boston: Beacon, 1973.

Giroux, Henry. *The Abandoned Generation: Democracy Beyond the Culture of Fear.* New York: Palgrave MacMillan, 2003.

———. *Fugitive Cultures: Race, Violence, and Youth.* New York: Routledge, 1996.

———. "Teenage Sexuality, Body Politics, and the Pedagogy of Display." In *Youth Culture: Identity in a Postmodern World,* edited by Jonathan S. Epstein, 24–55. Malden, MA: Blackwell, 1998.

Glen, J. Stanley. *The Recovery of the Teaching Ministry.* Philadelphia: Westminster, 1960.

Goodman, Paul. *Growing Up Absurd.* New York: Random House, 1960.

Greene, Maxine. *Teacher as Stranger.* Belmont, CA: Wadsworth, 1973.

Groome, Thomas. *Christian Religious Education: Sharing Our Story and Vision.* New York: Harpers, 1980.

Hall, Edward T. *The Silent Language.* Greenwich, CT: Fawcett, 1959.

Harris, Maria. *Teaching and Religious Imagination: An Essay in the Theology of Teaching.* San Francisco: Harper and Row, 1987.

Hauerwas, Stanley and John H. Westerhoff, eds. *Schooling Christians: "Holy Experiments" in American Education.* Grand Rapids: Eerdmans, 1992.

Havighurst, Robert J. *Human Development and Education.* New York: Longmans, Green, 1953.

Heifetz, Ronald A. and Marty Linsky. *Leadership on the Line: Staying Alive through the Dangers of Leading.* Boston: Harvard Business School Press, 2002.

Herberg, Will. *Protestant, Catholic, Jew: An Essay in American Religious Sociology.* Garden City, NY: Doubleday, 1955.

Hoge, Dean R. et al. *Vanishing Boundaries: The Religion of Mainline Protestant Baby Boomers.* Louisville: Westminster/John Knox, 1994.

Hoge, Dean R. and David A. Roozen, eds. *Understanding Church Growth and Decline, 1950–78.* New York: Pilgrim, 1979.

Hutchison, William R., ed. *Between the Times: The Travail of the Protestant Establishment in America 1900–1960.* New York: Cambridge University Press, 1989.

Jacoby, Susan. *The Age of American Unreason.* New York: Pantheon, 2008.

Kohlberg, Lawrence. *The Psychology of Moral Development: The Nature and Validity of Moral Stages.* New York: Harper and Row, 1984.

Kozol, Jonathan. *Savage Inequalities: Children in American Schools.* New York: Crown, 1991.

Lanier, Jaron. *You Are Not a Gadget: A Manifesto.* New York: Knopf, 2010.

Lave, Jean and Etienne Wenger. *Situated Learning: Legitimate Peripheral Participation.* Cambridge: Cambridge University Press, 1991.

Luther, Martin. *The Small Catechism.* http://www.cph.org.

Lynn, Robert W. *Protestant Strategies of Education.* New York: Association, 1964.

Mahan, Brian J. et al. *Awakening Youth Discipleship: Christian Resistance in a Consumer Culture.* Eugene, OR: Cascade Books, 2007.

Males, Mike. *The Scapegoat Generation: America's War on Adolescents.* Monroe, ME: Common Courage, 1996.

Martin E. Marty. "The Establishment That Was." *Christian Century,* November 15, 1989, 1045.

McGregor, Wynn. *The Way of the Child.* Nashville: Upper Room, 2006.

Mead, Margaret. *Culture and Commitment: The New Relationships Between the Generations in the 1970's.* New York: Anchor, 1978.

Mercer, Joyce Ann. *Welcoming Children: A Practical Theology of Childhood.* St. Louis: Chalice, 2005.

Miller, Bonnie McLeMore. *In the Midst of Chaos: Caring for Children as a Spiritual Practice.* San Francisco: Jossey-Bass, 2007.

Moore, Mary Elizabeth. *Ministering with the Earth.* St. Louis: Chalice, 1998.

———. *Teaching from the Heart: Theology and Educational Method.* Minneapolis: Fortress, 1991.

Moran, Gabriel. *Showing How: The Act of Teaching.* Valley Forge, PA: Trinity, 1997.

Morton, Ralph. *God's Frozen People. A Book for and about Christian Laymen.* Philadelphia: Westminster, 1965.

Neibuhr, H. Richard. *Faith on Earth: An Inquiry into the Structure of Human Faith,* edited by Richard R. Neibuhr. New Haven: Yale University Press, 1959.

Nelson, C. Ellis. *Where Faith Begins.* Richmond, VA: John Knox, 1967.

Osmer, Richard Robert. *The Teaching Ministry of Congregations.* Louisville: Westminster/John Knox, 2005.

Palmer, Parker J. *The Company of Strangers, Christians and the Renewal of America's Public Life.* New York: Crossroad, 1989.

Parker, Evelyn. *The Sacred Selves of Adolescent Girls: Hard Stories of Race, Class and Gender.* Cleveland: Pilgrim, 2006.

———. *Trouble Don't Last: Emancipatory Hope Among African American Adolescents.* Cleveland: Pilgrim, 2003.

Phillips, J. B. *Your God Is Too Small.* New York: MacMillan, 1961.

Piaget. Jean. *The Language and Thought of the Child.* 3rd edition. New York: Routledge, 1997.

———. *The Origins of Intelligence in the Child.* New York: Routledge, 1997.

Powell, Arthur G. et al. *The Shopping Mall High School: Winners and Losers in the Educational Marketplace.* Boston: Houghton Mifflin, 1985.

Purnell, Douglas. *Conversation as Ministry: Stories and Strategies for Confident Caregiving.* Cleveland: Pilgrim, 2003.

Putnam, Robert D. and David E. Campbell. *American Grace: How Religion Divides and Unites Us.* New York: Simon and Schuster, 2010.

Reisman, David. *The Lonely Crowd: A Study of the Changing American Character.* New Haven: Yale University Press, 1965.

Richter, Don. *Mission Trips That Matter: Embodied Faith for the Sake of the World.* Nashville: Upper Room, 2008.

Robinson. John A. T. *Honest to God.* London: SCM, 1963.

Roof, Wade Clark. *A Generation of Seekers: The Spiritual Journeys of the Baby Boom Generation.* San Francisco: HarperSan Francisco, 1993.

—————. *Spiritual Marketplace: Baby Boomers and the Remaking of American Religion.* Princeton: Princeton University Press, 1999.

Roof, Wade Clark and William McKinney. *American Mainline Religion: Its Changing Shape and Future.* New Brunswick, NJ: Rutgers University Press, 1987.

Sams, Ferrol. *The Whisper of the River.* New York: Viking, 1986.

Seymour, Jack. *Contemporary Approaches to Christian Education.* Nashville: Abingdon, 1982.

—————. "The Untried Curriculum: The Story of Curriculum Development for Protestant America." In *Confrontation Curriculum,* edited by R. Harold Hipps, 11–26. Nashville: Christian Educators Fellowship, The United Methodist Church, 1982.

Seymour, Jack, Robert O'Gorman, and Charles R. Foster. *The Church in the Education of the Public.* Nashville: Abingdon, 1984.

Skocpal, Theda. *Diminished Democracy: From Membership to Management in American Civic Life.* Norman: University of Oklahoma Press, 2003.

Smith, Huston. *The Soul of Christianity: Restoring the Great Tradition.* San Francisco: HarperSanFrancisco, 2005.

Steinbeck, John. *The Winter of Our Discontent.* New York: Penguin, 1995.

Tillich. Paul. *The Courage to Be.* New Haven: Yale University Press, 1952.

Tracy, David. *Plurality and Ambiguity: Hermeneutics, Religion, Hope.* Chicago: University of Chicago Press, 1987.

Turkle, Sherry. *Alone Together: Why We Expect More from Technology and Less from Each Other.* New York: Basic, 2011.

Turner, Victor W. *The Ritual Process: Structure and Anti-structure.* Chicago: Aldine, 1969.

Turpin. Katherine. *Branded: Adolescents Converting from Consumer Faith.* Cleveland: Pilgrim, 2006.

The United Methodist Book of Worship. Nashville: United Methodist Publishing House, 1992.

United Methodist Hymnal. Nashville: United Methodist Publishing House, 1989.

Volf, Miroslav. *Exclusion and Embrace: A Theological Exploration of Identity, Otherness, and Reconciliation.* Nashville: Abingdon, 1996.

Warren, Michael. *Seeing through the Media: A Religious View of Communications and Cultural Analysis.* Harrisburg, PA: Trinity, 1997.

We Have This Ministry: A View Toward Youth in the Church's Ministry. New York: National Council of the Churches of Christ in the United States of America, 1964.

Wenger, Etienne. *Communities of Practice: Learning, Meaning, and Identity.* Cambridge: Cambridge University Press, 1998.

Westerhoff III, John H. *Living the Faith Community: The Church that Makes a Difference.* Minneapolis: Winston, 1985.

—————. *Will Our Children Have Faith?* New York: Seabury, 1976.

Westfield, N. Lynne. *Dear Sisters: A Womanist Practice of Hospitality.* Cleveland: Pilgrim, 2001.

White, David. *Practicing Discernment with Youth: A Transformative Youth Ministry Approach.* Cleveland: Pilgrim, 2005.

Wimberly, Anne Streaty. *Soul Stories: African American Christian Education.* Nashville: Abingdon, 1994.

Winter, Gibson. *The Suburban Captivity of the Church: An Analysis of Protestant Responsibility in an Expanding Metropolis.* New York: MacMillan, 1962.

Wuthnow, Robert. *The Struggle for America's Soul: Evangelicals, Liberals, and Secularism.* Grand Rapids: Eerdmans, 1989.

Yust, Karen Marie. *Real Kids, Real Faith: Practices for Nurturing Children's Spiritual Lives.* San Francisco: Jossey-Bass, 2004.